LIVING THE PRACTICE

LIVING
THE PRACTICE

COLLECTED WRITINGS ON THE
TRANSFORMATIVE POTENTIAL OF YOGA

SWAMI RADHANANDA

TIMELESS
2016

timeless books
www.timeless.org

© 2016 timeless books/Swami Radhananda

in Canada:
P.O. Box 9, Kootenay Bay, BC, V0B 1X0
contact@timeless.org
(800) 661-8711

in the US:
P.O. Box 3543, Spokane, WA, 99220-3543
info@timeless.org
(800) 251-9273

Design by Todd Stewart
Cover and author photo by Daniel Séguin
All essays first appeared in *Ascent* magazine, 1999–2009

Library and Archives Canada Cataloguing in Publication

Radhananda, Swami, 1941–
    Living the practice : collected writings on the
transformative potential of yoga / by Swami Radhananda.

ISBN 978-1-932018-37-0

    1. Yoga. 2. Spiritual life--Hinduism.
3. Self-actualization (Psychology). I. Title.

B132.Y6R26 2012   204'.36   C2011-908728-6

Printed in Canada
Interior: FSC® certified 100% post-consumer-waste recycled acid-free paper
Cover: FSC® certified 10% post-consumer-waste recycled paper

Environmental Benefits Statement

By using paper made with post-consumer recycled content,
the following resources have been saved.

trees	water	energy	solid waste	greenhouse gases
19	31,631	8	255	701
fully grown	litres	million BTU	kilograms	kilograms

Environmental impact estimates were made using the Environmental Paper Network Calculator.
For more information visit http://calculator.environmentalpaper.net.

MIX
Paper from
responsible sources
FSC
www.fsc.org   FSC® C014956

zero
100% carbon neutral

by Hemlock Printers www.hemlock.com/zero

Also by Swami Radhananda

Carried by a Promise: A Life Transformed by Yoga

Timeless titles by Swami Sivananda Radha

In the Company of the Wise
Time To Be Holy: Collected Satsang Talks
On Sanyas: The Yoga of Renunciation
Light and Vibration
The Yoga of Healing
Kundalini Yoga for the West
Hatha Yoga: The Hidden Language
The Divine Light Invocation
Mantras: Words of Power
When You First Called Me Radha: Poems
The Devi of Speech: The Goddess in Kundalini Yoga
Radha: Diary of a Woman's Search

Timeless titles by other authors

The Inner Life of Asanas by Swami Lalitananda
Inside Outside Overlap by Billy Mavreas
The Glass Seed by Eileen Delehanty Pearkes
Inspired Lives: The Best of Ascent Magazine edited by Clea McDougall
In Durga's Embrace: A Disciple's Diary by Swami Durgananda
Yoga: A Gem for Women by Geeta Iyengar

Table of Contents

5 HEART, DEVOTION, DIVINE MOTHER

Introduction

THE ESSAYS IN *Living the Practice* were written over ten years for *Ascent,* Yasodhara Ashram's yoga magazine. Between 1999 and 2009, *Ascent* was transformed from a small ashram journal into an internationally respected publication by a group of aspiring and inspiring people wanting to live yoga and connect with others who were doing the same. I became a columnist.

The magazine reached out and came back into the work of the Ashram with stories, essays and interviews from artists, writers, musicians, activists and yogis. We were introduced to many people who were living the same basic ideals. It stretched beyond "stretch yoga" into the heart of yoga – it presented yoga for an inspired life.

Each issue was based on a theme, and that theme became my practice. I chanted, read, spoke at satsang, listened to what was happening in classes and in our work at the Ashram. I wrote and gathered my ideas together. It gave me an excuse to go deeper into a variety of life events and learnings, and it gave me a point of concentration and observation. I followed the teachings to see how they would expand and contract in each theme that was presented.

Sometimes the spiritual path is difficult and sometimes it is joyous and sometimes we just have to keep on taking the next step. There are some basic events that happen in anyone going through the process of growing up spiritually. Writing each article asked me to look at these events as ways to understand the human condition through my own experiences, and to offer the teachings of yoga as a way to help.

The book has been divided into five sections, five recurring threads that we found woven through the essays: *Reflection, Mind, Body, Light* and *Heart*. Together they make a whole; each is part of the whole person, and that's what we teach at the Ashram.

Reflection brings daily life into a symbolic form that has more meaning. It gives you a place where there is no judgement, where you can be the observer of yourself. It's so important to write things down because going back over it, the learning comes alive and the memories are available and accepted as all part of the path. Reflection is a wonderful way to keep track of growing up spiritually.

What about the mind? The mind becomes a sacred tool if you can control it and use it for the purpose it is meant for – to guide you to a vast and open space and to break through the bounds of your limitations and desires. You want a mind that is clear, that can be quiet and calm and give you the space to allow intuition to

enter. The mind can become your very best friend.
The body is your temple. I like the idea that the body is woven into the elements. We're not separate from the trees, the animals – we're all made of the stuff of the earth and there's a wonder in that. Observing how the body works is a miracle. Each part of the body reveals a mystery and serves us so wonderfully – helping us stretch and dance and move and live and eat. It can be made very subtle, supple and strong. It can be the place where we invite the Light in.

Light. Light is the most subtle element of the Divine. It is around us, sustains us, creates us, protects us. The more we invite the Light in, the more we invoke it, the lighter we become. The lighter we are, the less concerned we are about the limitations that hold us back. We eventually find out and accept who we really are.

The heart cannot be forgotten. For me it was very important to meet the Divine Feminine in all different aspects – strong and soft. The images gave me something I could mirror and that I knew was readily available. The devotional part of us is an integral part of opening and surrender. If you are not devoted to the Divine, you are devoted to something else. You make the choice.

How do you live your practice? Start small. Make a commitment. Follow through. Keep doing it until it works for you. Test it out – don't just do a practice in your room. Try it in real-life situations. If you have something you need to address, do your practice, face the situation, notice what happens, and see the learning that comes.

You can always make use of practice. It's not something that sits in your room – it comes out into your life. You can bring the practices into whatever you do – cooking, gardening, driving your car, working, being with people. You are more aware of what is around you.

To transform your life, you have to have a goal or an inspiration, something that will turn your worldview. It's like an epiphany – a goal that you can't resist. Through your commitment, your practice becomes the process of making yourself into who you want to be. And you're in charge. It doesn't matter what other people say. If you have that inner knowing that there is something more for you, that you want a meaningful life, it will happen.

An ordinary life infused with practice and inquiry becomes a meaningful life. There are many questions in the book but let your own questions come forward. Think, relax, chant, do Hatha Yoga, remember your dreams, bring the Light into your days, do service. Expand the mind of yoga!

SWAMI RADHANANDA

1 REFLECTION, SELF-INQUIRY, WHAT IS THE PURPOSE OF LIFE?

1 At the Beginning

AT THE BEGINNING, when I first started to study yoga, I remember being stunned by the questions I was asked: Who are you? Can you take responsibility for your actions? Can you see how you have manifested your world? Do you see your selfishness? Questions that turned everything upside down, questions that have no answers or have answers so big that they can't be fully formulated.

I was thirty-six years old. I had two children, an unhappy marriage. I was stuck. How was I going to live in that, and how was I going to bring consciousness into my life, take responsibility for my actions? How could I think more deeply about the people I was living with, and how could I truly grow up and live my life with purpose?

I observe other seekers come to yoga for very similar reasons – they have a craving for connectedness and community. They want to know how to live together creatively and peacefully. They want to know what to do with their pain, how to approach the difficulties in their lives. It seems that everyone comes with a burden. Young people especially are pressured with many problems and forced identities. They wonder who they really are, where they fit and why these seemingly unfair things happen to them. An absent or abusive parent, poverty, death of a friend, drugs, broken relationships, pregnancies.

What does the heart need? The steadiness of the heartbeat keeps life happening. A steadiness of practice and self-reflection keeps Light and the spiritual life alive. Our birthright is to know that we were born of Light, that the vibration was somehow set in motion for everything to develop.

In this gift of life, we have been given an opportunity to learn. All of us define the meaning of our life through our own experience. Not just through theory, not through someone else's experience, but through our own understanding. In order to live life to its fullest, our experience of it has to make sense. The mind has a tendency to want everything to be black or white, good or bad. We demand that questions have answers and that the world be concrete, not subtle or complicated or inexplicable. But life is complex. No one has all the answers. Our questions and problems can become the teachings as we face our challenges. We have to live life to find out, and the tools of yoga can help.

Through self-inquiry we can crack the shells of our narrowly held concepts and find our strength of character. We also start to understand the symbolic meaning of life events. One student described her experience of reflective life as living in a poem – rich, deep, cogent and symbolically hers to understand. When I started to look at my life symbolically, I remember feeling how something wise inside of me began to come forward. It was someone I didn't really know at the beginning, but the relationship to that part of myself grew and continues to grow as I honour and appreciate the inner guidance.

Most people come to yoga to find what is missing from their lives. They are searching for a map or set of directions for how life is to be lived; they are seeking magic and meaning. To live life fully requires the desire to engage in the process of growing up. We can step out of the survival mode into a passionate interior life. Opening ourselves, we become real people, going beyond image and age.

You can find the place within where you listen to your own truth. Knowing from the heart brings self-confidence, acceptance and respect. Life is what we make it – it's a process of learning from our mistakes and joyous encounters. It's having faith to try something new. Even a little idea or action in a new direction has a great effect on old static concepts. There comes a point when an idea has outgrown itself and needs to be replaced. Faith and devotion are essential for this process as we face each challenge. We develop the ability to wait for the divine connection even if it looks different than what we expected.

It's been over twenty-five years since I started yoga, and this winter marks my ten-year anniversary as a *sanyasi* and the president of Yasodhara Ashram[1]. It's definitely not the life I expected, but in looking back through my journals I see over and over how the

---

1   This essay was originally written in 2003.

plan for this was drawn out in daily activity, dreams and thoughtful reflections. The path was there and it required me to put my full attention to those signposts, to listen intuitively, allowing the events to unfold and surrendering my expectations. As the path becomes clearer and clearer, I acknowledge the divine whisperings of affirmation and confirmation: "Keep going..."

2 From Earth to Heaven

WHAT IS THE POTENTIAL OF YOGA? In the West, most
people have a very limited perception of what yoga is.
Many are familiar with the physical exercises, but yoga
is not just a series of exercises to relax or to keep fit. The
physical dimension of yoga, Hatha Yoga, is just one tiny
part of yoga philosophy. Yoga can take you from where
you are now to liberation, from earth to heaven, from
the concrete to the very, very subtle. You may start out
in a yoga class practising asanas, but where will this
lead you?

I remember my first Hatha Yoga class, and the
first time I did *savasana*. I thought, "My god, there's
another level here." I went deeper and deeper, but
where was I going? I had never gone there before,
but I knew immediately that I had been searching
for this place.

There is a very specific kind of person who is
searching for spiritual inspiration, a person who is
searching for understanding when life doesn't make
sense anymore, who is looking for a way to live with the
complexities of life. Yoga's purpose is to bring us deeper,
to help us look at who we really are. When we are

open to learning, we can enter a place that hasn't been explored yet...a place inside ourselves.

You have to put effort into knowing your inner Self. The Self is a pearl of great price, a precious treasure that is not easily accessible. Yoga demands that you look at all the different levels and possibilities of life. A life of self-examination, discipline and practice may look like a more difficult life, but is the other way truly easier? Why wouldn't you be curious about yourself, about your potential?

Yoga is a holistic approach that brings together the physical, mental, emotional and spiritual. At the beginning, little glimmers of inspiration act as signposts, leading you out of ignorance, to more knowledge, awareness and power – not over people but over your own Self.

This approach may seem foreign to us at first, but if we enter deeply into any spiritual tradition – east, west, north or south – we will discover different symbols, different methods; but the essence is the same. In all the different traditions we begin the process of evolution by establishing a strong foundation that helps us face our life situations, then we make a commitment so that higher levels of consciousness can be developed.

For Westerners it is often hard to see the mystical possibilities of our own spiritual traditions. I was attracted to yoga because it was, on the surface, so far removed from the conservative church I went to as a child, with simplified stories and sad hymns. The foreign images of the East shook up my idea of divinity with an array of gods and goddesses. Yoga promised that I could experience the Divine myself. Through dreams, practice and reflection I became aware of the vast array of possibilities and attributes of divinity. The Divine was not someone else's idea to be planted in my mind. In yoga, I grow and evolve through a deepening understanding of the mystical in my daily encounters. My life is my unique path.

The Western challenge is to bring yoga into our daily lives. We can't easily do what Eastern tradition prescribes: sit in a cave, or wander India leading the ascetic life. We have to go inward, and that knowledge has to be brought out again. We need to transplant the seeds of yoga into our lives. How do the seeds of yoga grow in the world? The understanding that grows out of our practice of yoga can be put into action. We find like-minded people, take yoga classes, support each other, create a space in our homes to do our practices... so then we can go out to work, be with family, live in the world. And feel whole.

The world is an incredible place. It has such a rapid pace, there is so much change. Yoga helps you to find a way back to who you really are. The Self is timeless and knowledgeable. Start asking yourself the questions that you want answers to. Listen. There is a part of you that knows. Beyond the modern east-west-global fast-paced world, there is a part of you that can ask the question, listen and hear the answer. What is the purpose to my life? Who am I?

3 Compassionate Evolution

THE FUTURE OF OUR WORLD depends on bringing our
knowledge into action. As human beings, we are aware
enough to make choices that can affect our evolution.
We can question how to evolve toward being fully
human and ask: What is the purpose of this life?

Scientists can determine our physical roots from
stardust, cosmic particles that have knit together the
miracle of our flesh and bone and brain. The whole
world and everything in it – mineral, plant, animal,
human – is made of the same essential components.
I find that physical interconnectedness intriguing.
We are also interconnected on other levels beyond the
physical. As the world becomes a global village, can
we recognize this oneness on the subtle, spiritual levels
through kindness and peace? Can we find a path to our
cosmic roots, and become rooted in an all-encompassing,
compassionate view of life?

We are given hard lessons of survival on earth. We
have the option to imagine the worst, to use our speech
to emotionally inflame people's actions – or we can
approach life with a harmonious, sensitive response. You
can cultivate the positive attributes of kindness and love

by laying a strong foundation of understanding of your own life. The knowledge gained from personal challenges and victories will allow you to understand human nature, and this leads to kindness, and an acceptance of others. Life is a great teacher. If we don't learn life's lessons, painful situations will present themselves. Disasters pierce our mechanical behaviours, our unthinking ways, our inability to give back to life.

Can we rise out of our inert mineral state, our weed-like desire to take over in order to control and manipulate others? An intelligent attitude will encourage the cultivation of finer thoughts. When our mind has the capacity to ask the question of our life's purpose, we take responsibility to cooperate with our evolution and move beyond our mineral, plant and animal instincts. We need intelligent, mature, inspired solutions to the problems in our world, in our lives.

Yogis see individual paths of evolution in the same way as good parents view their children growing into physical and mental maturity. There is the desire to develop potential and rise above limitations. Evolution is mysterious and never ends; there is always more to learn. But the learning requires dedication in order to actualize it into life, in order to change and to become more of who you really are.

When I first met my teacher, her voice pierced through the layers of the habitualized life I was living, bringing at first a great sadness that I had not heard such words before. Her words pierced through and connected with that little bit of consciousness hidden within me like a seed, and the seed started to grow. There is something within each one of us that can be sparked to life under certain circumstances and can begin to grow.

There are many paths up the mountain offering different approaches to spiritual life, and each in its essence leads us from selfishness to a greater awareness of the Divine. Everybody is moving toward the realization of just exactly what and who they are. There are great gurus and examples of people who can incorporate what happens on the level of daily life with what is happening on many more subtle levels. They fulfill their potential and are helpful to so many people. Isn't that what we were born to do? To love and help others, to bring Light and goodness into the world? Can we evolve to the place where world peace is possible?

4 A Fine Balance

WHEN PEOPLE FIRST GO TO AN ASHRAM or a spiritual
community, they often think that they have to commit
fully, put on a robe and leave everything behind in
order to be spiritual. Really, what an ashram asks you or
inspires you to do is make a commitment to your own
evolution and unique path.

While you may not be ready spiritually or
practically to live in a spiritual community, you may still
benefit from coming to a place set aside for retreat and
study because there you can find ways of incorporating
a spiritual focus into your everyday life.

When I first started visiting Yasodhara Ashram,
I found that each time I came here I could bring back a
new perspective to my family and work. At one point,
I decided to do a mantra practice when I went back to
my home. I chanted ten minutes a day in a little space
I created for myself. It wasn't an intensive practice,
but changes happened in me. I began to question the
conventions of my life and gain courage to act in difficult
situations. At that time, I was also involved with a yoga
group that met weekly for sessions of ten weeks. Even
taking that little bit of time, one evening a week, helped

expand our consciousness. We found something of value together and wanted to keep it alive. Each time we began a new session we would write what we had learned so far and what we would commit to for the next session. We focused on our own reflections and spiritual practice. The commitment kept bringing us back to why we were meeting, to support the best in each other and ourselves.

I've lived in all sorts of communities throughout my life. I grew up in a large family, and raised a small family of my own. I've lived in a commune and I've lived in communal housing. So I thought I knew what community life was like. When I moved to the Ashram, I made a conscious decision that I was going to surrender to the community, but my guru said, "No! Don't surrender to the community. Surrender only to the Most High." That shifted my vision of community life. Something higher was connecting us all, and it was greater than people's personalities or agendas or even my own ideas.

People all have their own reasons for coming to live in a spiritual community, and most of us think we are prepared, but usually the experience turns our worldview upside down. Failure may be success if the lesson is to learn humility; learning a simple task brings self-knowledge. By using the community as a mirror, we learn to know our own minds and can proceed toward Light and wisdom.

There is a fine balance between the personal and the communal. We are independent beings, yet we are together in a community, and we have to learn to live on this edge. The human tendencies of procrastination, ambition and preferences need to be addressed in our personal and group work. Our divine spark is nourished and encouraged through community respect and personal spiritual practices.

It is that tension between independence and community, seemingly contradictory ideas, that keeps any community alive. Each one of us has to do deep work on ourselves and keep bringing that work back into the community.

The independence we want to foster is an inner strength – the ability to make decisions, to think clearly, to be courageous – rather than a selfishness or a desire to do things our own way. In a meeting where everyone had a voice, one comment was, "That was such a great meeting – not everyone agreed, but everyone listened." Community can help foster that independence, but it requires making a commitment over and over and over. When the commitment is made, the ashram becomes everyone's, and they care for and respect it not from rules but from understanding and love.

That is what community can do – it can support people's sincere ideals. It may not be comfortable at times, and at those times you need your heartfelt commitment to carry you through the highs and lows of spiritual life. If you go through a difficult period, do you have the determination to keep on and meet the test? When distractions come up, can you make your own decisions based on your ideals? If your commitment is ambiguous, it makes your decision harder. A firm commitment to the Divine is a powerful reality.

By keeping to my commitment, I build the

foundation to face whatever is on my path as I live in the ashram community. I was thinking of this the other morning when I walked around the enclosed garden. The day was sunny and the garden full of garden sounds. The ashram cat decided to walk with me too. As we came to a chattering chipmunk, she hesitated...and then kept on walking. Around and around she went with me, each time making a commitment to keep on.

5 A Life of Learning

WHAT DO YOU REMEMBER? Do you remember the good or the bad? How do you build a foundation on the things that you have done well and the things that you have learned? How do you recognize that Divine Mother has been with you every step of the way? I've been asking myself these questions as I gather material to write a memoir. I am going through my journals and my memories: all the things I've learned in my life, all the experiences I have had, the interactions and teachings, the people and the places. Looking back, I can see how it all fits together – from my experiences as a child to first discovering yoga to where I am today. I can see my life as a path that was started and traveled on.

Self-reflection is such an important part of yoga. It is said that consciousness knows everything but the mind can't hold all of that knowledge. It just gets little glimpses. So you need to put the glimpses together, keep gathering up the clues. Writing down your experiences helps you train the mind to concentrate and observe, and it creates a record of your own personal wisdom.

Perhaps you already keep a journal and want to find a way for writing to be a part of your yoga practice.

A powerful way to start a spiritual reflection practice is to create a dialogue or a conversation with a deity, a god or goddess you feel connected to. For me, it was Divine Mother. I would ask a question and She would respond, or I would write to Her, knowing She was listening. The intention of having a divine conversation makes the act of writing much more intimate and meaningful than just sitting down and writing the details of your day.

Instead of just writing what happened in your day, ask: What is important for me to remember about today? What did I learn? What did I observe? How did She appear? What was Divine Mother doing today in my life?

By using an image or creating a feeling of being with Divine Mother as you write, you help cultivate that wise, compassionate part of yourself. You write with an awareness that life is not all about the things you haven't done right but about what you've learned and the wisdom that is gained. There is a part of you that has collected what you need to know. There is something that is always working in us to build the foundation so we can take the next step. And sometimes you don't appreciate your own efforts – you feel guilty about something, or angry, or you say, "I can't do that because…" or "I can't say that about myself." Divine Mother is very accepting. She will respond from Her point of view, from the point of view within you that knows – what you've done and what you haven't done and what you could still do.

You can also bring writing into your Hatha, mantra or meditation practice. There is some powerful reason why you do a practice, otherwise you wouldn't keep on doing it. You are responding in some way to what it gives you, so collect that and make it evident to yourself.

Writing is a tool that takes you to yourself more and more deeply. Language brings in another dimension. Often a spiritual experience is more than the words can convey, but words still carry your experience and nourish you. By capturing something in words, you begin to see that they may have more meaning than you think.

If you are observing, concentrating, absorbed in something, you will remember that time and what you learned. Memory and learning are closely connected. It is a process of watching the mind and seeing how it works. As you work with reflection, you begin to see your life with a new kind of perspective – not what you've done wrong but what you are learning. And if you can remember that, it makes you more independent and strong. A sense of gratitude arises for all you have been given, and this feeling encourages and inspires you to keep going.

We want to be able to go through a life of learning. How do you preserve what you have learned from this life, maybe even to the next life? What do you want to take? What is the most valuable thing? The most precious things are in your mind, all those things that you have learned. Through writing, you take a pause, and store your learning. Just turn inward and see where that wisdom is.

6 The Story of Your Life

TODAY I RECEIVED TWO LETTERS – one very inspirational, and the other full of blame. I am always amazed at the timing of events like this, how these letters show me clearly the power of language – and its extreme range of both positive and negative impact. In yoga we want to learn how to bring the mind to its natural, balanced state, in order to hear the inner voice of wisdom. A statue of Kuanyin, with her hands at her heart in *namaste*, is a reminder on my desk as I write. She encourages a message of stillness and compassion.

We live in a world of words – from our own constant chatter to the outside, instant, up-to-the-minute, around-the-globe news chatter. Language often comes with a warning: "This may be disturbing to some people" – detailed descriptions of child abuse, the daily killing of war, and the politicians' slippery words that make reasonable discourse impossible. There are so many ways for words to disturb and hurt that we need to cultivate other words of power that bring harmony and peace.

Speech is an integral part of the process of spiritual development. People who have traveled the path before us have left instructions about how to achieve a greater understanding of what it means to be human. Their teachings have been put into sacred texts, making them widely available. We recognize the depth in these sacred texts, chants and mantras even if the words are foreign or seem beyond our understanding at first. They carry within them a sacred meaning that can be awakened through practices and training.

Just as we study the ancient texts looking for wisdom, we can study the texts of our lives. Through reflection we discover the potential for our own words to become sacred. Words have the power to tell and retell our personal stories. Recently in a workshop two of these stories stood out to me. One woman wrote about her life as a child during World War II – reliving the painful experiences but also seeing how she was a survivor. She recognized an inner strength that could propel her forward in her spiritual quest. By putting the old story on paper she could see how her life had changed, and she could update her self-image from victim to survivor. She was amazed at the help she had received over the years. She found room in her mind for gratitude.

Another man had a fear of groups from a terrifying childhood experience, and held onto that fear for years, unable to make the changes he wanted. He wrote the story of the young boy as if it had happened to someone else. He asked a group of his peers to hear the story he had written and through this process his mind could release the old story. The group was able to hear and support the young boy and understand more compassionately the man.

Affirming an experience through reflection, writing and speaking brings the words forward and dissolves the emotions that surround an event. This gives your mind – the interpreter – another way to understand the experience. The mind has a tendency to hold onto stories. Emotions and emotional words are the glue that keeps us stuck and contaminates relationships, careers and personal growth. Released from emotional interpretation, the mind can change its mind, allowing you to mature as you use different language to describe yourself and your life.

When we can reflect, tell stories, use our voice and ask questions, we can move away from old habits of speech that are emotionally embedded in the present and insert a new vocabulary that more clearly embodies who we are. The gift of a yoga practice is that we can see how we grow from ignorance to wisdom with the challenges and choices life brings. We need to know what we are practising, whether it is staying stuck or stretching toward our potential. We have a choice.

Expressions of deep yearning and knowing often come out as poetry and there is a subtle beauty and a resonance when ordinary words become the vehicle for finer feelings. Letting the heart speak requires us to suspend the analysis, keep the silence and wait for the response. Self-inquiry, the ability to ask questions and dialogue with the inner voice of knowing, brings a new way of expressing who we are. Through practice we can find the wisdom within. The ancient texts support our questing, but our own questions are the spark that takes us deeper into our own wisdom.

To practise studying the text of your life, here are a few exercises you can try:

1 Come to a quiet reflective place, using a mantra of your choice.

2 Write a story about an incident in your life from an early time. Distance yourself as if you were writing about someone else. Make it come to life.

3 Ask someone to listen to your story. Saying the words aloud brings more awareness of their power.

7 The Myth of Perfection

"Divine Mother holds two extremes:
maya and liberation."

                – Swami Radha

WE ARE CAUGHT IN *maya*, the play of our continuous
illusions, drawn into what is swirling and moving and
changing around us. In the fluctuations of this change,
we search for stability and security. We look for the
mythical perfect place outside of ourselves – the perfect
job, teacher, relationship, Hatha pose, body, lawn
– anything that seems normal, complete and looks as if it
will stay the same. When you think you've found it, you
can say, this is who I am, this is what I want, this is what
I can do.

We believe in a life-story. Taking the threads of
our days and weaving the dreams and dramas and images
together, we build this story. But what is real?

We often sense indications of a reality that is just
below the surface of the ongoing story of our lives. The
real is that magical combination of human and spiritual.
The real is experiencing the essence of who we are in the
present. We all have a wisdom within that connects us

to a more penetrating view of life and clarity about our purpose in it. The commitment to face your reality is a potent crossroad in your spiritual life.

But the myth of perfection is strong, and can stop you on your path, challenging your decision to go forward. When the desire for perfection is too great, we don't have easy access to our own knowing. We can't act; we are afraid to make mistakes. But we are human and learn through trial and error – it keeps us humble. When we keep the image of perfection – which on the spiritual path often manifests as fundamentalism or a holier-than-thou attitude – we forget our purpose as humans is to evolve and be compassionate to those around us. We lock ourselves into a prison of perfection in relationship, in work, even in our spiritual life. Looking at the facts can reveal how little we know about ourselves and who we really are.

We can make up some very creative ideas about who we are. We go out of our way to have the right clothes, the right kind of work, a perfect partner. We often define ourselves in relationship to other people. The other person reflects back what you want to be, a mirror of who you think you are. But being in a relationship can be challenging if you don't know yourself or if you project what you want onto another person. Maybe you want something that the other person can't give. Maybe you are so self-critical that you can't see yourself clearly. You need someone to reflect back at you so you can feel appreciated or so you won't feel lonely.

Also, with a perfectionist attitude, a little change

seems like a big change, so big you think it can never be done, or it takes a lot of redoing and revising and the results are slow in coming. Change becomes very difficult, and the main reason is perceived criticism from others, or even from yourself. Negative thoughts take hold and grow. "I am discouraged and struggling with blame...I'm trying not to give into the desire to criticize myself...the depression caught me...it's like a fog...I can't see what my mind is doing...it takes me a while to really get in touch with my emotional reactions...I want to hide from it...I feel caught." Criticizing yourself prevents you from making use of what you do know and limits what you can do.

Liberation in part is recognizing that negative concepts and habitual emotional strategies must die. In Eastern teachings death is part of the change of life. There are constant rounds of birth and death. At a point of near death your life flashes before you and you realize the pettiness of holding onto painful ideas and unresolved relationships that hold you back. It is as though the curtain of *maya* is drawn back and you gain understanding and decisiveness.

In the imperfect there is perfection. Often people don't recognize their own Light. When they begin to step over the hurdle of criticism and learn to trust themselves, life opens up. Recently an older student in teacher training felt that she couldn't teach, that she wouldn't be able to do the poses perfectly. But she followed her body as it was, drawing on her many years of wisdom, and she now radiates Light. Her students can appreciate what she has to offer because she has an understanding of how to approach them from her own experience.

The nourishment for continuing on the path is in the small details of quality and joy and usefulness in everyday life. By recognizing these details you will develop faith in the presence of the Divine in your heart. This deepening of faith helps in facing the reality of your situation.

There is a giving part in all of us, an expansive generous part that recognizes life and its challenges and doesn't back away from changes and commitments. By developing a foundation and learning about yourself, you are stepping forward on the path of liberation. Keep learning and be an inspiration to everyone.

8 Steps to Freedom

WE ARE FAMILIAR WITH MOMENTS OF FREEDOM, but we also know how it feels to be stuck, caught, as though there are obstacles in our way. We feel imprisoned by limitations. Limitations sometimes manifest on a physical level – inflexibility appears in our body or a rigidity of the mind – we keep bumping into ourselves and other people and things. Nothing seems to work. It feels as if the sky has collapsed and clouds are hanging around us, and our limitless potential seems far away.

The goal of yoga is liberation from all limitations. So how do we overcome limitations? Look what happens when you do Hatha Yoga: a stiff and inflexible body will stretch, release and relax. In the same way, if you use the other tools of yoga you will stretch your mind and bring your essential self into the Light. Watching your mind, chanting a mantra and meditating can give you the space and the perspective to see the obstacles in your path: Where are you and what is restricting you? Is it hard to get up each morning? Are you obligated to another person? Are you afraid to take on a responsible position? Is it difficult to change a habit?

We have the ability to grow out of our limitations.

The process starts with the willingness to see a limitation as the indicator that something needs to change. We don't have to stay in confinement or pain. We can get to the root of a limitation in life, be it another person's expectations of us or our own expectations of ourselves and other people. I have seen many people take steps to challenge their beliefs about who they are, what they are allowed to do and what their life is supposed to be. A woman who was attached to her pain said, "I want to face my depression so I can grow into my potential and have no regrets that I didn't take the opportunity." In recognizing her limitations and choosing to move through them she took many little steps: making decisions about her medication, acting on her dreams, having a regular yoga practice and noticing how she used her time. Each step changed her perception of what life was offering her, who she was, what she knew and what she could do. Gratitude and inspiration replaced the depression as she learned to trust herself, and she voiced this. In a simple, sincere way she brought positive actions into her life.

A man who didn't believe in himself said, "I want to face the fear of being on my own for a while to develop inner strength." He took a first step and went through a time of confused thoughts and ideas about what he really wanted to do. This brought up the issue of loneliness. Each step as he moved into his aloneness brought a different perspective and also support from sources he hadn't been aware of before. It was as if in taking the first step to change there was encouragement to engage in his process and find his inner spiritual strength. Change is a natural part of life and change requires that we take risks and face fears. If we don't risk, we can never transform fears into courage or our obstacles into strengths. Through the experience we learn that fear, risks and mistakes are all part of life and can lead to inspiration. Each step we take shakes up our life so that we have a new perspective and more possibilities.

A risk in a relationship could be to support the best in the other person even if it means letting them go so that they can do what their hearts desire. Accepting the change may mean seeing the illusion of the relationship dissolve or feeling the pain of loneliness that is there.

A risk in reaching your own potential may be to fulfill a dream of travel or schooling. If your interest is music, go beyond fantasizing. You could buy yourself an instrument – learn, make mistakes and put yourself to the test. By learning to play you will find out where it takes you. Life is risky and at some point we need to move out of the comfort zone to face life courageously, give ourselves the freedom to act and take responsibility for the learning that comes with that choice.

Reflection and spiritual practice enable us to challenge our ideas, to be thoughtful and self-disciplined. Integrating what we learn about our inner selves into our outer lives makes us stronger and gives us more choices. The energy that we once put into our limitations is freed up and directed toward cooperating with our ideals.

Once you taste freedom you want more. You know it is time to face the unknown. You want to dig deep for the gems and the gold and not keep moving on from distraction to distraction. Life really is what we make of it and the more we can see that, the more we can create a fulfilling life. There will always be another step. Be ready to explore and take a risk. It is a worthwhile and exciting journey to freedom.

2   MIND, INTELLIGENCE, LEARNING

1 Turning the Mind

ABOUT TWENTY-FIVE YEARS AGO OR MORE, I was given a small blue teapot with dark blue and gold flowers on it. The person who gave it to me knew I liked to drink tea. It is an ordinary teapot, but one that has served me well. Tea always tastes special from this pot now. Through care and years of service, the ordinary teapot has become sacred. For me it represents the ability of the mind to turn toward the sacred and become a useful instrument.

My mind's original training was to worry, criticize, wander or want to get things right. No one ever told me that the mind could be a vessel of sacred things. So when I was introduced to simple practices such as watching my mind, chanting mantra or visualizing Light, I recognized that my mind had other abilities that could lift me up rather than pull me down. It's like pouring something white into a dark place, pouring milk into black tea, until there is no tea left, only milk. My mind was a vessel and I could choose what to put into it.

Any person, with the right service, care and appreciation, can change his or her mind to become a precious vessel. So many of us are just ordinary people looking for a better way of life, a healthier mind and a healthier body. We often see our mind as a chaotic or dark place, but the natural state of the mind is actually one of space and light, so we have to look at what we've filled our minds with.

It is important to remember that there can't be a line between where the mind is and where you are. Everything is your mind, how you look, what you do, what you say. Your whole environment is your mind. Mind is not the invisible thing that we think it is. Begin to observe yourself. What words do you choose? Do you use speech to reinforce the negative in yourself? Or do you use it to create a positive atmosphere? How do you treat your body? Do you bring awareness to it, sit with it, stretch it, move it, care for it? Do you push your body and throw it around? Do you ignore it?

Everything is symbolic. You are giving a message to yourself and to others through your appearance, your actions and your speech. These are all indicators of where your mind is at. The events of the day will allow you to see your mind at work. Stop and look at what is happening in your life; you are somehow contributing to that situation.

There are usually two things that will spark a resolution to change the mind, a traumatic experience or an inspirational example. Sometimes you have to come in contact with a life situation that is difficult or threatening. Life will bring you an opportunity to change, but it is often painful. The other way you can come to change the mind is if you see someone else changing, and you desire to be that way too. That desire or that trauma can bring you to a different place, and you will want to know more. That will be the beginning, when you realize that there is something bigger and more important than you are.

I remember at one point when I first began studying my mind, there was a moment when it felt as if the rug was pulled out from under me. Everything I thought my mind was, I realized it wasn't. I had a strong sense that there was something much more to life than what I had created for myself. All these things we build up in our lives aren't real; they are mere constructs. We have all created a world for ourselves through imagination, expectation and choices. But all those constructs of how we think we should live our lives will only serve to limit us. We all have those moments of clarity when the rug gets pulled, but more often than not we rush back into our old constructs. The mind is a comfort creature. What do you really want? The challenge or the comfort?

If you take up the challenge, how then does the mind turn into a sacred instrument?

First of all, it has to be a conscious desire, a clear decision that you are going to change. An ideal to change the mind can be set out. Say to yourself, "This is what I am going toward." It takes determination and sincerity.

The other part to consider is that changing your mind takes a long time. It is like the teapot: the change doesn't just happen the next day; it is a seasoning process. Over the years the teapot absorbed the tea essence, the fresh boiled water, the care. The teapot adjusted to the purpose it was given. There is a real commitment involved.

The mind is known as the sixth sense. When you turn the mind to the sacred, you will begin to sense that there is another dimension to ordinary life. You can see the Divine manifest in the ordinary. When a life is lived in a sacred or devotional way, it can be recognized by others. There may be a new calmness, or an engaging quality that wasn't there before. Each mind has its own idea of what is sacred. In the West devotion isn't part of our daily culture, but when the mind is given the opportunity to be devotional or to be a sacred instrument, it has the ability to transform.

I can look back over my last twenty-five years and now see the serious intent of my mind to uphold a sacred position. I can see how I began to look at my life, other people and opportunities in a different way. Even the disasters became blessings. I learned how life experiences were my lessons and gifts. This is what evolution is all about: being given the life secrets and giving back. Like the teapot being filled to be emptied again.

2 The Promise of Practice

A STORM ROARED THROUGH THE ASHRAM the other night, full of flashing lightning and howling winds that uprooted trees. The next day a rainbow appeared and the sky was beautiful, soft and glowing. The forces of nature can be both violent and beautiful. How do we make sense of these contradictions? We live on this earth, a place that is very concrete and often full of destruction and despair, yet we are striving for a spiritual life that is very ephemeral and full of hope.

Lately I have been rereading *Tibetan Yoga and Secret Doctrines*, a series of Buddhist teachings translated by W.Y. Evans-Wentz. When I first read them, I had just begun my yoga practices, and the words struck my heart. The one line that has stayed in my mind ever since is this: "Having obtained the difficult-to-obtain, free and endowed human body, it would be a cause of regret to fritter life away."

What action is needed to make our life worthwhile? There is a need for spiritual discipline and devotional practice. However, an important aspect of any spiritual practice is taking action at the end. You have to say, "I am going to put this to work in my life." That's the part we often forget about our practices, whether it be Karma Yoga or Hatha Yoga, meditation or mantra. How can this really become part of my life?

In order to say, "I will take responsibility for my ideals and ethics; I am going to put these spiritual values into my life," you may have to change what you think being "spiritual" is. Often people do a practice, and they think that's all there is to spiritual discipline. You do a practice for hours and hours, but you may not really know what you've accomplished. We need other people and we need other situations to test it out. Are we truly patient? Are we truly caring about somebody? How do you talk to people, work with them? Can you take other people's opinions? Can you open your mind to a place where you are receptive to another idea, or are able to see that someone may need your help?

We live in the world with other people and it is usually the small things that interfere with the calm practised mind and cause a storm of emotions: the reaction to the mess of dirty dishes someone else left on the table, the inopportune time someone barges into your workspace, the driver in the next lane who doesn't signal. They all expose your ability to control your mind. Everyone meets a crisis – from little disturbances to larger life events. The effort we put into reflection on these events helps us to understand our reactions and to change our way of approaching people consciously.

Leading a spiritual life, however you establish that – in an ashram, at your workplace, in a yoga group, in a family – is going to positively affect the world around you. You create places of Light, places where people are intentionally bringing the Light to earth.

It takes strength and courage to go against the mainstream of life, which is now unfortunately mired in apathy and comfort. It takes courage to say: I want to reflect on my life; I want to clarify what my words and actions are. In this way, leading a spiritual life can be a political act. You are making a statement that you want more than a life that is driven by social pressure, instincts and common habits. Can you take a stand in your life, or for a principle that you believe in? Can you build a commitment to something other than yourself?

We are looking for the practices to make changes and take action. We are looking for how the mind works, how the heart opens. It always has to come back to the connection within so that we can see the reflection without.

A lightning strike will light up the whole sky and a small candle will light up a very dark room, so there is hope with each effort we make to incorporate Light into everything we do. The vibration of spiritual practice is a blessing and an inspiration to all. Having obtained the difficult-to-obtain, free and endowed human body, it is up to us to accept the challenge to change, to open our hearts and minds, and to live our lives fully.

3 Intelligence

EVERY DAY OF YOUR LIFE YOU GET UP and "go to work."
For many of us, this means going to a job at a specific
place and time where we deal with pressures, ideas,
worries, habits, ambition, laziness, money, lack of money
and many other things. Instead of getting caught by
all these things, the mind can learn to use them in an
intelligent way. Instead of creating a routine that deadens
the mind, an intelligent approach can revitalize your
work and help you recognize your target, so you know
you are living your life with purpose.

When you start to look at work in the larger
context – that your work has to do with becoming your
real Self – things start falling into place. You can see
that each day offers opportunities to do the work of
becoming the person you want to be, whether you are
in a stressful office environment or in a relaxation class
at a retreat centre. Understanding why you choose to be
doing what you do can help bring meaning to your life.
You may start to wonder: Why am I here? What is my
real work? What am I preparing for? In the Bhagavad
Gita, Arjuna, the spiritual seeker, is posed in a battle
against his family, friends and teachers. Arjuna is an

archer, skilled in the art of hitting the target – the target
of life. When he prepares to enter the battle he becomes
despondent and throws down his bow. Krishna, his
divine charioteer and advisor, tells him to stand up, to
act as a warrior, to do what he has to do. The message is
for all of us: we have to do what we are here to do. This
means facing the battlefield of daily life with the courage
to do what is before us.

The bow is a very precise tool. Practice and
strength are required to be skillful with a bow and arrow.
Clear sight is needed to see the target without being
distracted by emotions or by what surrounds the target.
In a battle, your life could depend on your ability to use
your bow. In daily life, your spiritual purpose depends
on your ability to use your intelligence.

As humans, we have been given the gift of
intelligence. In order to understand the situations we
are engaged in, we must pick up this precise tool of
intelligence and use it. What is the symbolic message
in your work? What is being offered that can help you
understand what you need to work through in this life?

The hidden messages of your work start to be
revealed when you look at your actions, your intentions
and your ideals. The meaning of your life reveals itself
very precisely and uniquely in everyday situations. When
you begin to reflect on these situations and develop a
symbolic language, you will start to realize the different
roles that you play and the different personalities that
you possess.

Once you become an active participant in your
own life, you have to confront all the personality aspects

that helped you survive in the past. When you see your life as something you have created, you must accept responsibility for it. You will start to recognize that you have exactly what you need. Just as Arjuna has the bow and the skill to use it in battle, we each have our intelligence and the power of reflection to meet our challenges. All the essential ingredients are present in this mixture we call life. When we face the challenges, we are led to a connection with our higher purpose. A sense of gratitude begins to enter the mix when we recognize that the challenges are blessings in disguise.

Ask yourself: What is it I want my life to be? What atmosphere do I want to create around myself and my work? Life offers more if we have an awareness of others, and if we act with care, quality, commitment and responsibility. Intelligence can help us make changes in our attitude. Life invites challenge; for many people, the challenging situations are the ones that force them to turn to the Divine. Intelligence invites change, and it is the intelligence within you that will also help you face the next change in your life.

Many people, when overwhelmed by the challenges and changes of life, revert back to old ways of coping. Like Arjuna, they become depressed and throw down what they know. Instead, you can ask: How did I get here? What can I do? Use your intelligence to face the difficult situations. The ability to reflect on daily events and activities will allow you to gain an understanding of how the rest of your life can be lived with purpose and a commitment to the highest intelligence.

4 Searching for Silence

IN THE TEMPLE, which sits overlooking the lake, light streams in from all the windows and there is a sense of deep quiet. We chant *Om*, our voices blend, come in and out of sound to a place where the note begins to vibrate in the atmosphere. All of us in the temple become part of the note. Then, as if we make a collective inaudible decision, we know it is time for the chanting to end. The *Om* fades and there is silence. We have created a silent space that is very rare. I recently read about a scientist who travels around the world searching for silent spaces. He has found that there is very little natural silence left on our planet. Each year the encroachment of mechanical noise comes much closer. A noisy world is at our doorstep. A noisy world is also in our mind.

Silence can be a beautiful and peaceful thing, but for many people trying to survive in the world of noise, silence is threatening. Often there is a sense that there is something lurking just below the surface in our minds that we don't want to look at. Or we wonder what people are thinking about us if they are silent. We are looking for rejection or acceptance from others and talk is the usual way we get it. There is usually a reason we set up the barrier of noise – often silence has been used as a punishment, maybe someone was angry or upset, or silence is used in judgement.

It is interesting what will arise in silence. The outside noises may fade, the mind may quiet down, but the issues that need sorting out in the mind rise to the surface. There are certain things the mind holds onto: criticisms and limiting key sentences that hypnotize people into thinking that they will never amount to much; they don't fit in; they will be hurt or rejected; they are dumb; they are different from everyone else. Criticism and worries become immediate in the silence, so you want the silence to be filled. Immediately. Silence is the first place you have to pass through to find out what is happening in your mind.

Silence allows you to watch your mind and become aware of the thoughts that you may be acting on unconsciously. When you see the thoughts, you can make a conscious choice to act on the thought or change your mind, instead of going along with the noise. I have seen people who don't want to look at themselves keep going until something happens that makes them stop – a sickness or an accident – but it gives them that reflective, quiet space where they can face what is difficult in their mind. We each have a unique purpose to fulfill in this life and inklings can come in those quiet moments. I remember the first time I chanted alone in the prayer room here at the Ashram. I could feel the history of many people who had practised in the same way in the same place. It became unusually quiet. As I walked out into the sunlight, the silence stayed with me. A butterfly landed on my shoulder and was very still. That was the first time I realized I could find my own potential in silent spaces.

There was the feeling of limitlessness. I became aware of the preciousness of life, what life had offered me in the past and what is possible in the future. My attitude could change. The key sentences can be positive, I can generate gratitude, I can keep watching my mind, I can find a quiet space each day to reflect. When I started to look for those silent times in the day they started to appear. The small still voice is available and prepared to give you what you need to know about yourself and what you already know. The teachings reside in silence.

Silence has a profound quality that words often can't convey. There is a story I like of Rama and his teacher Vasistha. Rama asks Vasistha a question but he replies in silence. "I ask but you do not answer," says Rama. Vasistha responds, "It is not because I could not answer that I was quiet, but because silence was the answer to that question."

I find as I grow to trust that silent state of mind that I can use it to listen and be in difficult situations. In the silence, sequences of activity begin to unfold, the answers come. The mystery of silence intrigues me. It seems we create silence but it also seems silence is waiting for us to enter. We have many ways to enter by bringing it into the mind through stillness, breath, relaxation, sacred sounds, acknowledging the power of gratitude and appreciation, being with like-minded people or being alone. There is something so powerful about how the mind and the body respond to the depth and space of silence. We should start searching for silence.

5 Clearing the Air

THE ATMOSPHERE IN THE ROOM was tense and charged. Two people at our meeting were having a heated exchange, their voices loud and full of emotion. Both said that something had been building between them for a while but it hadn't been discussed. This blow-up was set off by a simple comment, but this comment opened up the storm. We've all been in similar dramatic situations that are like living though a thunderstorm with clouds rolling in overhead. We can feel the shift in the atmosphere, then see the lightning and hear the thunder.

The pressure that brings atmospheric change comes when actions and speech are incongruent. The tension in our meeting grew because speaking up was being avoided at all costs. But when the atmosphere in a room changes like this, the power of speech, thought and emotion become evident. The undercurrents of unspoken thoughts or spoken jibes and jabs have an incredible force to affect the environment in which we work and live. Often these undercurrents build and become stress, burnout or illness. Tensions need to be brought to light in order to clear the air. We rarely know the extent of our mind and its workings, and we know even less about the mind of another person. So as we enter into a situation with another person it is as if we are entering a minefield where an explosion can be triggered by almost anything. Who knows what will set off an emotional response? A person may start to withdraw and appear unhappy. When approached, the person says, "I am fine. I'm doing my best." We have learned to silently cope rather than to address an emotional or unknown situation.

Undercurrents thrive because many people fear facing someone who could be extremely emotional or judgemental. Usually this is because there has been some shattering experience in our lives. For example, many people from alcoholic families remember unpredictable disturbances and want protection and order. Others remember situations in which they were teased, criticized, bullied, abused or ignored, making them cautious about entering anything emotional. When you are not on firm ground, doubt comes in. A storm of thoughts starts up: I won't be listened to; I don't do anything right; no one is receptive to my ideas; they can do it their own way.

If we want to live together in an atmosphere that supports honest work on ourselves, then we have to start by looking straight on at our fears, beliefs and preferences. It is through exploring our own mind that we have the opportunity to grow and trust, instead of being stuck in an old response or habit. Building up habits in the mind is like piling junk in the environment we live in. When we litter the landscape – our backyards, highways, parks – everyone can see it. When we litter our living or working space with negativity, others can sense it. We are more porous than we realize. We affect and are affected by those around us, so we need to develop the courage to clear the air; we need a daily practice to keep the environment clean and healthy and vibrant.

Spiritual practice allows us access to our own minds. Observation and reflection become essential. There are always ups and downs in us, in others, in life because life is like a wave – it is not straight and logical. This constant change brings tension and pent-up energy that can go in any direction. The energy is neutral, but allowed to run wild it can destroy. Gathered and directed, it can be managed and creative. Your personal world has to be controlled. A fit of anger can destroy what you claimed as friendship. We don't have the power to change the entire world but we can begin to change our own mental world, which we are continuously creating.

Airing our feelings can bring a bigger picture to the stormy situation. Sometimes just asking a question is a way to release the pressure. What is happening? Gathering the facts reroutes the imagination into a more realistic picture of what is taking place. The two people in our meeting began reflecting and talking openly about the incident that had occurred. They came to see the causes and tensions and began rebuilding ways they could relate to each other. To find resolution is often simple and liberating. Carrying around underlying tensions is much more painful.

The reality of the atmosphere we live in is that

it brings fog and clouds and sometimes builds to a thundering roar. Our spiritual practice is the way we live through these interactions, refining and clearing a space for the higher qualities of gratitude, loyalty, humility and respect for all life.

6 Stepping out of the Classroom

MY FIRST EXPERIENCE AS A TEACHER was in a two-room school in Lillooet, BC. I stood at the front of the class and asked the children to sit up. The whole class as one entity immediately sat up very straight. They all looked at me, waiting for the next instruction. A question registered in me at a deep level: What was I to do with the power I had been given in this classroom? What was my responsibility?

As a teacher, I see that as soon as I sit in the chair, students will often give their authority to me. People want a dividing line between the teacher and student, a line that says the teacher knows more. They want someone to tell them what to do. Yet a good teacher should be searching for ways to foster independence instead of dependence. A teacher's job is to see the potential in people and want to draw it out.

Through teaching I have learned how each mind is unique. I also realized that there is no dividing line between teacher and student. What is a teacher? A teacher is also a learner, a learner of minds. I am learning; they are learning. We learn together. We all have a duty to help each other, like a big sister or brother stepping ahead first and helping others take the next steps.

When I was a young student, I was drawn to windows – looking out. I wanted to sit in the rows by the windows. I wanted what was happening inside to connect with what was happening outside. What we were learning in the classroom didn't have any relationship to my life. There is nothing we did in the school that related to the environment in which I was living. We learned things in our workbooks; the workbooks were marked. It was what someone else thought I should know. It had no real relationship to my mind, my life outside the classroom.

We have been conditioned to think of our lives in classroom boxes, in neat rows. Our everyday life is segregated from the life force that wants to truly know our Selves, our minds and our purpose. How do we connect with this spiritual life? People tend to keep it separate, have a different classroom for each part of their life – one for work, one for family, one for spiritual practice, one for recreation – but no connection is made between them.

What each person needs are the tools to explore the mind so that they can find the potential within themselves. We often learn on an intellectual level, but there is another kind of understanding that comes from what we call the heart. Teachings or spiritual tools allow access to the heart by revealing obstacles that have kept us in safe, mechanical ways of living, just like those neat rows in the classrooms.

The teachings are available to all who are sincere;

the path is open to everyone. The basic principle involved with teaching is to ask what is best for each person. We all have what we need within ourselves. The task is to unwrap ourselves from the covers of conditioning, asking, "Why do I want to wear this wrapper as my real Self? It was a protection once; someone put it on me or demanded it from me. But now I have other choices."

That's what a teacher does: she tries to get you to remember what you know, put it into the context in which you are living. Then your life can expand. Spiritual tools can open minds to a broader perspective, put life into a context in which we begin to feel gratitude for what we've been given, because things start to make sense. You will discover that there is a purpose and a reason to life. You start to learn about your mind and how it creates the world that you live in. The inner life reflects the outer life.

Life is inconsistent. There is no right or wrong, this or that, up or down, yes or no, in or out. Often there are no answers. This goes against what we have learned and adapted to through education. These dualities are extremely limiting. There is a bigger context to every situation. The more possibilities you allow yourself, the less confusing and chaotic life will seem. There are millions of possibilities and many answers to every question. It is not right or wrong, but what is appropriate for the situation, what is serving the best in yourself and others as you see it. Even if you make a mistake, you will learn from that mistake.

Question life around you, learn about the place

of questions, and the freedom of having no answers. There is a place inside that can remember, that knows. There is an inner teacher that can discover the teachings. A spiritual teacher is only a conduit for the teachings, an inspiration and example on the path. In my teacher I saw something I wanted – a straightness, a light and an intelligence. Often a teacher is someone who can see another dimension to life, who has had an experience of the Light and how it works. They bridge the gap, make a connection between the sacred and the everyday, not leaving it at an intellectual level.

The question of teaching really comes back to the questions we can each ask ourselves: What do I do with the power I have been given as a human being to think and to make choices? How do I envision the future? How can I become more considerate, kind and helpful? What life do I want to create for myself? How can I step out of my old concepts? What is the purpose of my life?

7 Learning To Teach, Teaching To Learn

THE LINE BETWEEN A TEACHER AND A STUDENT is much more fluid than we think. You can't be a teacher unless you are a learner. There has to be a willingness on both sides – one to give and one to receive. And the process never stops; there is not one point when you are only a teacher. And there is not one point when you are only a student. We all hold knowledge, and we all have something to learn.

There is a natural desire in us to share what we know. Years ago, when I worked at a daycare centre, I would observe the children as they played or painted or cut paper – they were so happy when they figured out how to use the scissors! And if another child wanted to know how to cut a piece of paper, someone showed her. Then there would be two of them who knew how to cut paper. The children would show each other how to do new things because they would be so excited about crayons or paper or cutting…whatever it was.

As we grow older, obstacles often enter into this fluidity in the form of competition or a desire for a perfect teacher to tell us what to do, or an overpowering will that wants to control what others learn.

So it is very important that we ask ourselves: How can we keep this spirit of sharing as we learn to use different tools, the tools of yoga?

One way is to recognize the qualities and conditions of being a teacher and being a learner. Learning is a discipline in engagement; you need to put in the effort. Knowledge is not something that can be handed to you. You have to do the practices, ask the questions and find out for yourself. You can't have expectations of what you are supposed to know. You have to start somewhere, you have to accept where you are, and the next step will open up.

When you start teaching, you find out how much you have learned. And with that knowing comes the responsibility to bring the teachings into your life, knowing that you are an example. As a teacher you can only teach from your own experience: If you don't know something, say you don't, and there is more truth and integrity in the teaching. For a teacher, there is a mirror in the student; for the student, there is a mirror in the teacher. We can be constantly asking of one another: What do we need to learn, what do we already know, and what can we share?

My teacher often talked of having "spiritual companions" on the path. She appreciated having students she could talk to who were committed and deeply interested in yoga. My own experience of teaching is a process of learning to trust the tools that have been given to me, and that the people who come to me are unique and intelligent. As a learner, I am constantly aware of what I don't know, and what a gift it is to be able to go deep into my humanity.

When you see how far you've come, gratitude emerges and you'll want to share what you know. If you truly understand your process and have your own insights, you can give back. How do we express that kind of gratitude?

When I think of where I was when I first started studying yoga, and how my teacher gave me the tools to change my life, I want people to have those same tools – so I teach from that place.

In this age of wireless worlds, having an opportunity to learn from each other is a wonderful gift. Creating a relationship with another person in a meaningful way – through telling life stories and listening deeply – has an immediate impact. We are on the same planet, a small place in an ocean of space, and we need to learn from and help each other, understanding that we are one in the Light.

8 The Subtle Path of Kundalini

"She is as subtle as a spider's web." '
— *The Serpent Power*[1]

THE SPIDER'S WEB IS TUCKED VERY NEATLY in the curve of a wisteria vine. Only when the sun shines on it at a certain point in the morning can I see it plainly from the kitchen window. Jiggling sometimes as the spider steps across it or waving with a breeze, the web is becoming more and more hidden as the leaves begin to fill in.

The power of Kundalini can be found in everyday life, and when this happens the mysterious becomes evident, like finding the web in moments of sunlight. The Kundalini system is subtle. Kundalini transformation is not necessarily a flash and crash of spiritual highs. Every one of us, whether we know it or not, is on the path of evolving our consciousness. Kundalini Yoga offers a way to access awareness of the Divine. To learn anything new is a process. While the tendency is to intellectualize the symbols, powers and

---

1   *The Serpent Power*, Sir John Woodroffe (Madras: Ganesh & Co., 1958).

meanings of Kundalini, we have to experience this yoga to understand it.

In Kundalini Yoga, we start at the first of the seven steps and begin to build a strong foundation. The first *cakra* relates to the element of earth – a very concrete form. We live, we die. Energy is neutral. Life presents many choices of how we use this energy, but often we get caught up in life's busyness and forget our true purpose. We are born and want to survive. There is an inherent biological force that wants to create. Can you use this creative energy in a more subtle way? The powerful forces of sex, competition, ambition, success and love will arise. These forces can take you away from finding out who you really are.

The first *cakra* gives us the choice of whether to identify with the gross aspects of life or with the Light. The Kundalini system has the subtle ability to transform your life. The path to Higher Consciousness starts here. The second *cakra* takes us into a more fluid element of water, which symbolizes the imagination. Here we need to practise directing the imagination, so it doesn't follow the well-worn routes established in the mind. The mind is like a garden in which anything can grow. It's up to you what you allow to grow and what you weed out. You also need water to cultivate a garden. A mind needs the water of inspiration and joy.

You can imagine anything you want to cultivate in yourself. Water flows to fit any container. It is easy to imagine all the bad things, but where do you want to put your energy? There is a well of endless energy that can be visualized and shaped into countless options. You have choice. You can see the choices people make consciously or unconsciously by their actions and speech. What kind of person do you want to be?

The third *cakra* governs emotions and is the fire of our life. Once the fire wheel starts spinning we all recognize the queasy feelings of upsetting emotions. Emotions keep the wheel going around and they can become very addictive. What are emotions for? Emotions are an indicator of unawareness, that there is something that needs to be looked at. Usually there is a hardened concept of what life should be – it has been fired by the emotions like clay in a kiln. How do you make your mind more flexible instead of going immediately to an emotional response? A new focus has to be gathered. Emotion can also translate into passion, a passion to lift out of the routine.

Before we get to the fourth *cakra*, at the heart, we come across a tiny wishing tree. If you really set your heart on your higher goal in life, your commitment can lift you out of the merry-go-round of the first three cakras. The heart in most cultures has the connotation of love, but it also requires courage to open. Clearing away resentments and grudges from your heart can open a space for finer feelings. At the heart, we get a glimpse of a sacred place within us, and it is here that we are born again as a spiritual aspirant. The experiences of the heart have to be strong enough to support us in our self-development because the path offers many challenges.

By making a heartfelt decision to continue on the path, we enter the fifth *cakra*, which is the gateway to liberation. The throat symbolizes this very narrow passage as a link between the head and heart. To listen to the heart you need to set aside old ideas that live in the first three *cakras*, creating space for new ideas to come in. Willingness is needed to carry on with your commitment to attain higher consciousness. After years of controlling, manipulating and gratifying your desires, you need to start practising surrender. Through the renunciation of desires, the Divine can enter your life in a more efficient way. By stepping out of your own concerns, the opportunities for selfless service become available.

The sixth *cakra* is the mind, still and reflective. The mind doesn't have any light of its own, much like the moon, but when the mind focuses on light, it becomes a powerful interpretive instrument. We often don't realize the potential of the mind, because we fill up its natural open space with junk. In order to realize pure mind you have to cut through the fantasies, the overlay of others' opinions, and search through your cherished beliefs for the truth. It means taking responsibility for the life that you've created. You can create and destroy worlds like the spider weaving and reweaving her web. At this point in the Kundalini system you have to practise what you've learned through all the different worlds in your life. You have been able to follow your intuition to this point, and many concerns will drop away. The work doesn't get easier, it becomes more subtle. Conscious evolution is ongoing. The seventh cakra is beyond the mind. It is indescribable.

Kundalini is a multidimensional yoga that touches on every element of human life. If you are a learner, it will keep you very busy. Many use Kundalini energy for their own gratification, but this leads to confusion and pain. We can only unite with Higher Consciousness through a process of refining our five senses and recognizing their power, accepting what life offers as learning situations and bringing quality to our actions. We know so little about ourselves and our potential. Kundalini must be experienced, and the experience brings knowledge.

This morning, I looked for the spider web in the vine, but it was gone. What remains is my focus on the symbol of the web. I have seen many other webs in curious places. My eye is becoming accustomed to the search. This search is the essence of Kundalini Yoga – becoming attuned to the subtleties that create and change our world.

3 BODY, BREATH, SENSES, HEALING

1 The Body of Teachings

HOW IS THE BODY essential to spiritual evolution? We
need the body to measure our growth. When we were
young, we would mark our height on the wall. As we
grow in awareness and take steps toward enlightenment,
often other people notice something different and say,
"You look lighter," or "You look transparent." I know
that feeling. I know that I have changed because I've
relied on the messages from my body, my mind and
my dreams.

As we start to do spiritual practices such as Hatha
Yoga, or chanting or reflection, we start to discover that
the body is more than what we usually think it is. The
body is not just the animal part; it is not just something
to be fed and clothed. It is a receiver. When you are
very quiet and relaxed, you receive; you can open and
surrender to what is. If you become very concentrated,
you can focus on energy in its most subtle form of light,
and make it vivid and real, and connect with it. The
more spiritual practice you do, the more Divine Light
you can receive. The body can reflect the Light, hold the
Light, gather the Light. As you practise, you are able to
live with that energy consciously and harness it. It has a

specific purpose. The power is available but it is not ours, although we have an incredible ability to connect with that power.

In my very first Hatha class, my body was stiff yet the movements were familiar somehow. The poses took me inside and there was a connection. It was a connection to a knowing part that began to speak to me in images and dreams. It spoke in expansion, breath and movement. The connection seemed familiar, yet I'd never done yoga before. Yoga was more satisfying than anything I had ever done, and also more challenging. I remember the relaxation in *savasana* at the end of that first class. It seemed strange to have lived so many years without ever having totally relaxed before. I could feel layer after layer release, and I had a sense of going deeply into myself. I knew, at that point, that there was more to me than I had realized before – I didn't even have words to describe it.

Relaxation is the first step to surrender. If I breathe and relax my body, I tune into another rhythm of life. There is something bigger happening – something living and breathing, like the moon and the tides, the days and nights, and the seasons. As I relax I gain an awareness, too, that I'm being supported and looked after. In relaxation everything in me is relaxed and quiet, still and breathing. The heart has its own rhythm. In this place of stillness I have access to many other levels, such as joy and harmony, peace and well-being. I also have a knowledge that it is not my energy, that there is something keeping me alive. This is the Cosmic Energy, the energy of the source. It is like going to a well and drinking from that source. I used to think I didn't have time to relax. Now, if I feel anxious or stressed, I take fifteen minutes to relax. And because I do a relaxation practice every day, the body and mind are ready for it and look forward to it with pleasure. Through relaxation my body is satisfied and energized.

How does the practice of relaxation fit into spiritual life? I don't think you could receive instructions or teachings unless you were able to surrender and accept what is. Most people can't surrender. They want to do what they want to do, and they want to do it now. The practice of having a teacher is to acknowledge and accept that there is someone who knows more than you do. That's hard for most people. But if you want to know something, you have to find somebody who knows more or who has gone through it before. When you find that person, you have to acknowledge, "Okay, I'm here to be taught. I'm ready." They will ask, "Can you hear what I'm saying?"

If you can't even listen to your own body, if you can't stop your mind from going around in circles, how could you listen to the guru's instructions? A guru is always testing. In schools we are tested for intellectual capacity but gurus test for sincerity and willingness. Swami Radha tested me by asking me to do what I thought I couldn't do. Since she asked me to do it, I tried my best. It's a feeling of leaping, almost like leaping off a cliff. Metaphorically this is what any teacher asks you to do with your concepts. An anxious mind or a resistant mind or an intellectually arrogant mind is very hard to deal with in a classroom or in life. There is no room for anything new to come in. It's already filled up.

So how do you surrender? You can learn it first through the body, where you have a very concrete way to feel and understand surrender. When I see that I receive benefits from physical surrender, what happens if I surrender mentally? What about spiritually?

I often use the expression, "a body of teachings." I think of a body, all the different parts – arms, hands, feet, legs – working together for one purpose. Yoga is a system that works toward another kind of purpose, evolution. The teachings don't live in the air or in a book. They have to be embodied. They have to be brought to life and lived. Our bodies have to open to the teachings through our actions, through our speech, through our interactions, through a new way of being. We live in a very three-dimensional world and we usually don't go beyond it. It's like the fish in the pond; every now and then they will leap out into another element, but basically they stay in the pond.

Some traditions dismiss the body. But I think that everything can be lifted and refined and made more subtle. It is important that we accept the body and use it as the vehicle for consciousness. We can think of life as a school where we have to go through different grades or different lifetimes to become perfect. Or we can use the idea that we are like a container or chalice that will hold the divine nectar. You wouldn't put what is most precious into a dirty container. You wouldn't put crystal-clear water into a muddy old mug. You would clean it out first. This process of clearing out the dirt is what the spiritual path is about.

If you see how most people use their bodies – for self-gratification of desires, greed, cravings – you can also see that they do not recognize what they already have. What would happen if they were given something more precious? Can we ask for more when we don't even appreciate what we have?

Treat your body with kindness, care, acceptance, consideration, Light. Treat others with kindness, care, acceptance, consideration, Light. Constantly feed the best in yourself and the best in others. It starts with your own body.

2 Holding a Pose

THE BODY IS A GOOD PLACE to start a spiritual practice because of its potential to change and show concrete results. By exploring the physical practice of Hatha Yoga, you begin to recognize the balance, strength and firmness of your body. From this foundation you can develop a trust in yourself to discover new possibilities not only in your body, but in your emotional, mental and spiritual attitudes.

A Hatha practice is really a beginning step. We practise asanas, postures, positions. Our bodies loosen, our breath deepens, our minds expand. The next step is discovering how we bring this experience from our practice to our lives outside the classroom. Can we learn to embody the essence of a pose and bring it forward into daily life, into our relationships, our families and our work?

For some people, the Tortoise pose is a challenging pose to go into, but the Tortoise can teach us much about patience. What does it require physically? You enter with care, moving slowly, with consideration, to warm up the body. You need to be patient to extend the stretch, relaxing while staying engaged.

The pose starts when you stay with it. As you learn to hold a pose, there is a knowing you can draw on. When you accept where you are in the Tortoise pose, then you can meet the place of limitation and begin to discover that something moves even in the stillness. You don't need to strive to meet any expectations. You are in a position to use the stillness for self-investigation. Staying with it reminds you that you can approach the truth about yourself by degrees.

Now translate your learning as you enter into a challenging situation in your daily life, whether at work or in your family. Bring in what you know from the Tortoise about patience, flexibility, care and consideration. For example, you are in a meeting, and the agenda is set about a project to complete. The purpose of the meeting is clear, yet there is an underlying tension that starts to develop between several people, that takes away the focus and keeps bringing it back to a personal level. You may feel your shoulders start to hunch and stiffen and your lower back begins to ache. Is this the position you want to take?

Remember back to the Tortoise pose. Can you take the pose mentally into the meeting? Can you keep an inward focus on patience and stay relaxed while being stretched? By staying engaged with what is really happening, there is an opportunity to ask questions and the undercurrents can clear. The truth in the moment can be recognized.

By staying with the situation and working through challenges that arise you can move beyond self-imposed limitations. Slowly you may notice that other people start to listen to each other and respond with care and consideration. And as they see their positions differently, the focus in the meeting returns to the project.

We have so many expectations of what we should look like or how we should be in any situation, especially if we are trying something for the first time. Often there's someone right beside us who looks as if they can do everything better or faster than we can. There is an expectation that we can do the perfect pose, be the best person on the job. There are many expectations, but what happens if you strive to get into that pose or strive to do the work better than the other person? Usually only a lot of pain. What is needed is the concentration of self-discipline where all your movements of the body and mind are considered and skillful. It may not be a perfect pose or solution but it is respectful.

When you are respectful to yourself, then you can begin to see that the body is a spiritual tool that responds to subtle influences: the breath stills and allows the mind to focus; mantra calms and softens from the inside out; Light charges the body and allows it to lighten and stretch. These influences help in any situation and bring you back to the purpose of yoga, which is to recognize your essential self, your ideals and your unique path to liberation.

Our bodies carry us forward into every situation in our life. By going into the poses you gain strength, flexibility, patience, acceptance, discipline and openness. Coming out of the pose, the continuation of the practice is to bring what you have developed forward and not collapse back into an old way. You can build the bridges of lived experience between your physical/mental/ emotional/spiritual worlds to keep the practice honest and evolving.

In keeping your commitment to your divinity and your ideals, you begin to master the pose and you go deeper into the subtle levels of understanding where you meet intuition and inspiration. Here is where the understanding of spiritual practice becomes evident, in the moments of joy and harmony within body and mind, and with the people around you. Yoga becomes a dance, a fluid movement through the ups and downs of our life, a way to approach our life with creativity, a way of healing and health and a way to make space and nourish the Light within.

3 Breath, the Invisible Work

SWAMI RADHA ONCE WROTE THAT, "As you keep practising, the channel will become clearer. This is a form of selfless service." In my own practice, I've been investigating what this could mean. How could my commitment to a personal practice open me to more clarity? How does being clear help me in my work with others? After thirty years, I still go back to the basic practices, the building blocks of yoga: breath, visualization, relaxation and concentration. The simplest exercises access the power of more complex practices.

Breath is a good starting place, because it is so available. There are all kinds of pranayama exercises you can do, but you can begin with the simple practice of observing your breath. You don't need anything else. Breath is always available; it's the rhythm of life. You can see different rhythms in your breath when you are in different states of mind, and if you turn your awareness to that interplay, you start to learn what's happening between body and mind. You begin to realize how breath can be calming and connecting, and can bring stillness in a moment.

You can also begin to question your practice: you question because you are questing, you are looking for understanding; you are not just doing the practice mechanically, pretending that something is happening. It has to be real. So you can ask: What is it that comes in on the breath? What is the life force? When I stop breathing, what isn't there for me? What am I connecting to when I breathe?

Breath can enter very deeply into your body as it supplies every cell. Can I stay with my breath and expand it by bringing in the mantra or visualizing the Light with the breath? Is there an awareness of tension and relaxation, depth and fullness? When I can build my awareness on many different levels, I can shape the responses of my mind and emotions, building a firmer foundation for self-control. There is space for the possibility of being free from many limitations and eventually reaching a place of peace and harmony. This is helpful for the health of the body and mind.

You can follow the breath's pathway in, and access a very deep, precious part of yourself. We have a visible part of us, the concrete and physical, and we also have this other part that is invisible. With an awareness of breath, we let the body and the mind become more familiar with the inner, less obvious place, where an inner knowing and clarity can come through. There is a freshness of insights that makes me realize that breathing is a devotional practice as well.

When there is clarity of mind, selfishness disappears. There is another part of us that can arise in that clear space. One that is intelligent and able to listen to someone else and give them space, that is very helpful in a work situation, a family situation or an emotional situation. So in that clearing of the mind, we connect with some inner wisdom and can let go of resistance, which opens us to possibility. It's like the way the breath goes: it inhales something and it exhales something. Breath is a practice of being able to let go and a practice of being able to draw something in.

Everyone in the world is breathing the same air, and if we can't work together and be generous because we're too afraid that there won't be enough air for us individually, what happens? It puts up barriers between people, barriers created out of fear and greed. When we actually begin to think of other people and do work for the joy of doing, and doing what needs to be done, then there's something that starts to happen – we are working together, for a purpose. And our work becomes meaningful.

The work is never only physical work. It's also the invisible work. A practice manifests in many ways, in our physical work, in our daily tasks or studying, but there is also the invisible work of breath and Light, of clearing the mind, connecting with our inner wisdom, an ability to listen, of letting go of resistance and selfishness. A simple practice such as breath may not seem like much but, for me, it is the saving grace in my work. I prepare my work, but I also prepare myself with the practice. With this in mind, I know that I am doing the best I can do, and that I give everything I can.

Even after years of practice, the power of breath still inspires me. And the more I practise, the more I see what it gives me, and the more I can do in my work with others. By breathing, I can make something softer happen. So then the simple practice of breath really becomes a selfless service.

4 Gateways of Perception

I WALK IN THE CEDAR FOREST up the hill from my house every day. It is like entering a different culture, a world where I can absorb silence and marvel at the astonishing beauty of the trees – some fallen with new ones growing out of them, others tall and straight, others survivors from a fire long ago. The smell of the forest's rich earth and greens comes into me and I connect immediately with a whole spectrum of life of the forest. Sometimes I glimpse a deer or a grouse or a path I've never taken before. Yesterday there was wind in the trees, and today it was absolutely still.

Our sense perceptions are our gateways to the world around us but we don't usually give them much thought. I can walk into an environment that brings my senses to life, I can appreciate the richness of the forest, but how can I also use my senses to cultivate stillness, alertness, wonder and awe within myself? The practice of yoga is the practice of cultivating, not only the body, but also the five senses and the mind. It is important to look at our senses – smell, taste, sight, touch and hearing – to become aware of their depth and power and also how they can take us to the next level in our spiritual development.

We can take the sense of smell for an example. How often have you smelled something and immediately had a memory triggered from that smell? You smell menthol and suddenly remember being three years old with a bad cold and your mother rubs Vicks into your chest. Another person may remember being in a room alone in a hospital, sad and worried. Smell sends your mind back into the past where a unique imprint was made. The smell of perfume reminds you of an old lover; the smell of a certain food reminds you of distant family dinners.

When we are not aware of where the odour is taking us, then we may be judging a new situation based on old survival needs. If left undeveloped, the sense of smell encourages sensual responses to food and sex that are stimulating and exciting. With refinement comes a connection with a different sensitivity. Can the sense of smell be refined and subtle enough to bring the remembrance of the Divine from the fragrance of sandalwood? Can a fragrance arise from an elevated state in your meditation or connection with the Light?

Each sense can be examined by asking: What power does this sense have over me? Is my perception true, or am I acting on impressions taken in by my senses in the past? We have an enormous ability to heighten our awareness and make choices. When we practise Hatha Yoga, we bring our attention to the body; it is exercised and becomes flexible and relaxed. We bring attention and concentration to the mind and senses for awareness and strength. Through cultivating the sense perceptions we will realize the choices we have depend on how we use these powers.

When we watch our mind we see the busyness and restless habits; when we focus the mind we experience the openness, wonder and beauty that are available within. Through meditation or spiritual practice you can guide the mind to single-pointedness and draw the senses in to cooperate and create a spiritual atmosphere.

Prepare a special place for your devotional practice. Carefully choose what is most beautiful, most meaningful, most intriguing, that reflects the inner atmosphere you want to develop. Bring a subtle image into the mind and body as a way to concentrate the senses. Use your imagination to focus the mind on a point of light, to see the light, feel the light, and to have the light penetrate every level of being and consciousness. Place your hands over a candle, feel the warmth, then touch each of your five senses. You can ask, "May all of my sense perceptions be purified by Light."

We can also use the senses, and the power of imagination, to help us in our spiritual practice as a way to enter into a meditative state. When you desire peace, visualize your favourite place and go there whenever you want. Place yourself in a wonderful, beautiful garden – see your favourite trees and flowers, smell the most beautiful scents, feel the warm air, hear the birds sing. It is a very simple practice, but it is a way to understand the power of the senses to create a peaceful place in the midst of the complexities of daily life. Sitting quietly, constructively using the senses, is one way to relax and to rest your central nervous system. The mind is absorbed, contained and focused.

As we cultivate the senses and refine the mind, we are able to see the patterns of the intangible in our actions and speech, the interconnections of the senses and the Light. We can use all the parts of our mind to remember our purpose, to move from the gross level of being to a deeper connection with our spiritual life. We can live a life that's kinder and gentler, and more considerate to ourselves and to others when we know that the true function of the body, the mind and the senses is to lead us to the Divine.

5 Intimacy & the Strength of Selflessness

SINCE NO HUMAN ACTIVITY IS ISOLATED, developing quality and cultivating the senses is essential in a sexual relationship. Each partner is affected on all levels – from the physical to the more subtle interplay of forces between two minds. The essential energy is neutral and has the possibility of our true potential. Sex is one of life's most powerful energies and remains the basic way that new life is created.

Sex is a bonding and creative function that has become a big business with an emphasis on selfish pleasure. Our society is saturated with highly charged sexual images, the media exploits and dehumanizes sex, the medical industry has pills for women not to be fertile and for men to be fertile longer. There are societal pressures on everything from how much sex you need to be happy, to what sexual preferences are culturally acceptable.

There is often a disconnect between the reality of the creative power of sex and the abuse of this power. Many people experience sex and sexuality as traumatic. Numerous studies have reported that one out of four women have been sexually abused. Many women and men were abused when they were young and powerless – usually by someone close to them, either a relative or a friend. Often the incident and feelings are hidden even from themselves because it is so degrading and painful. Given these experiences, it is easy to be confused about the meaning of safety and intimacy.

Instinctively, the senses grab for pleasure and satisfaction without any thought of the other person or the consequences. When someone is concerned with fulfilling his or her own needs and doesn't consider the other person, this affects us on a deep level because of our expectations of love. We have to understand what sex is and that it cannot fulfill all of the desires and expectations that are imagined. When there are so many mixed messages, we become disconnected from who we are and want to be.

People come to yoga to find the answers within themselves. Yoga is about bringing balance to body, mind and spirit. You start out as who you think you are and slowly begin to find out who you really are. Self-discovery is important because it lets you access your own source of energy and inspiration that is not dependent on someone else.

We can all start to clarify for ourselves, Who am I? Personal insights promote strength and clarity. By being strong within yourself, you don't need to bend to the societal pressures of sex, sexual identity or body image. You can determine where you find pleasure, what you can do, what you can give and how you want to deeply connect with others.

Selfless service is at the core of yoga; it is a practice of giving back and putting your ideals into action. When you know yourself, you have the ability and responsibility to utilize that knowledge to bring quality to all of your activities. In selfless service, you think of what needs to be done so that others benefit. It lifts you out of emotional neediness and brings feelings of connectedness and joy. All actions are motivated by desires, so it is helpful to desire to do your best and dedicate what you do to the Most High in yourself. You see in small increments the freedom that arises when you are not in the grip of desires. Your heart feelings are more expansive.

In recent experiments neurologists have been studying what goes on in the brain when test subjects placed the interests of others before their own. By scanning the brain they have observed that the area in the primitive part of the brain that usually responds to food or sex lights up on the scans. It could be that thinking of others is a basic necessity, an old survival method that can be revived in our relationships, our families and our communities.

Yoga is not practised alone. We do yoga in classrooms, with our families and in our communities. The spiritual practices have a profound intimacy that goes to the core of being human. By exploring the meaning of life experiences, the difficulties, challenges and victories, people of all ages and relationships can acknowledge their inner wisdom and learn from each other.

When we practise selfless service, we can become

more open to real intimacy. We can learn to listen, to respect and to recognize the preciousness of each life. We can see for ourselves that intimacy is not always through the lens of sex or the body. By shifting the focus away from societal sexual demands, we can give ourselves time to renew and to heal. Life is not easy and it is great to have companions on the path. We need this creative energy for a life of quality, and to have Light and a safe haven in a spinning world.

To investigate the power of image and self-knowledge, check your habitual way of looking at yourself. Looking into the mirror, what do you see? Listening to your name, what do you hear? Can you change your perceptions? All these investigations give the opportunity to realize that "knowing myself will make me free." You become knowledgeable as you lay a foundation, becoming aware of your illusions, desires and emotions so you can make wise choices. You are not the body. You are not the mind. You are Light eternal.

6 A Space for Peace

THE MYSTERY OF LIFE tends to draw people to yoga.
There's something beyond what we know and what
we can see. How do we find that out? How do we
experience peace and oneness with the Divine when
we are rooted in a daily life that takes its toll physically,
mentally and spiritually?

Through our five senses we experience the world
around us. Each sense has a power that is undeveloped,
and this power can be cultivated and refined by
practising awareness. For example, with our sense of
sight, the eye registers the visual impressions and the
mind interprets those perceptions. There are filters, such
as emotions, that prevent us from seeing clearly. There
is a need to develop an awareness of what happens when
we see. How much do we really see and know?

The Headstand is an excellent Hatha Yoga pose to
explore what we think we know. It puts you in a position
that allows you to see your world and your perceptions
differently. As you build strength and confidence in
the pose, you can become relaxed and attentive to
the effects on your body, mind and emotions. Look
around the space you are in and be aware of how it

looks to you from this upside-down perspective.

You can apply this to another level of your sight by looking with your mind's eye at your life and some of your cherished beliefs. Then take the opposite view and see how you feel. This practice develops the courage to challenge yourself and to really find out your own truths.

By turning perceptions upside down, the very fine subtle intuitive thoughts are no longer overpowered by strong passions or urges or doubts. Our intuition can guide us to the next step in our spiritual development. Then the passion that drives us is the truth. We want to know the truth and to experience the peace that comes in those moments when we've connected with something that's true for us.

In the Headstand, we can see that a good foundation is built: our heads are planted firmly on the ground, while our feet stretch to the heavens. In yoga, your head isn't in the clouds: the inner work becomes very practical to your everyday life, in the way you learn about yourself, the way you learn to access the knowledge you have within yourself. Knowledge is different than the intellect that thinks it knows. You have a fountain of knowledge within and you have to go and find it.

Life is your adventure, your investigation and your chance for self-discovery. What you learn about yourself becomes an enormous source of energy and inspiration. When you have glimpses of your inner Light, you create the desire to find out more, to understand more.

Spiritual life is all about inner work and becoming conscious. To be conscious is to know your nature, to understand your motives and impulses. This knowledge gives you confidence to discriminate and make decisions. The more you know yourself, the freer you will be. The discipline of yoga – the postures, breathing exercises, relaxation and reflection – transforms us into a receptive tool, allowing our intuition to unfold the mystical aspects of life.

In contact with life's energy there is a vision that is beyond the intellect and ego. We get caught in limiting ourselves with habitual thinking, but we are limitless when our heart desires to be one with the Light.

We often go looking for the great spiritual experience – something fantastic that will set us free – but there is nothing more fantastic in the whole world than peace and truth.

To help you explore the potential of the Headstand, take these exercises into your next practice:

1 Go into the Headstand. All movements have significance in this posture. Bending over to place the head on the floor is symbolic of humility. The feet and legs are lifted off the ground, surrendering the security of the earth. Maintain full attention in the completed pose. Connect with the Light or a spiritual thought. Discover the support and basic nourishment that come from a higher source. Ask yourself: What happens if my world is turned upside down? Write your observations and insights.

2 Sit in a comfortable position, in a quiet place, and become still. Fill yourself with brilliant white light. In your mind's eye, see your navel. Form a clear picture of a silver disk (the moon) on top of your navel. When the picture is clear, feel the coolness of the disk and watch it move in concentric circles, mingling pleasantly with your body heat. Expand the concentric circles as you add PEACE to your focus. Fill your body, mind and space around you with peace, and then let it reach out to others and the world.

7 Sacred Ground

I HAVE A LITTLE APRICOT TREE in my yard that blossomed this past summer and gave fruit for the first time. At first the tree blossomed, then tiny green balls developed and started to grow. I waited and waited for the apricots to ripen, and it took a very long time because the tree grows the kernel first. Only after the inner seed is developed do the green balls slowly start to flesh out and turn shades of orange. At last they offered the sweetest fruit. I thought this was a very good way to think of our own development: you have to put a lot of effort to strengthen your kernel, your centre, so you can plump out in the Light and be able to offer something back.

Nature teaches us about time and patience. Seeds take time to germinate and grow, and even the most difficult soil has a life force. As we grow, our self-inquiry and life experiences allow us to develop the ethical and moral ground on which we stand.

At the start of this growth, often there is fear rooted in the need to survive or to hold onto the security of the familiar. What is needed is discipline and commitment, as well as a release of rigidity and routines. Real growth demands that we go beyond the comfortable, as familiar patterns block the way for new perceptions. Expectations and reality, setbacks and victories are all part of growth. Each seed sets itself where it lands and goes through the process of growing and resting as it matures.

When we begin to study the ground we live on, our own earth, it's amazing to see how creative it is. Take the amazing array of life forms that grow here – everything is so astonishingly beautiful and complex. Earth is also part of the symbolism of the first *cakra* in the Kundalini Yoga system; it is the creative element and our foundation. The *cakra* holds the essence, the tiny seed of Light inherent in our human birth. This cosmic energy is what enables us to live, grow, think and transform.

In spiritual life we make a connection between the earth and the Divine – the two work together. I once dreamt that my guru came to me and said, "If you want to kiss my cheek, you have to have your feet on the ground." The message I took from the dream was that if I wanted to come close to the Divine, I had to be grounded and practical. This meant studying, reflecting and practising so I could be rooted in the teachings and grow from that place. We often imagine or hope for a spiritual life or personal development, but how do we really live it? How do we create sacred ground?

The earth creates and supports life because it has all the elements that we need to survive – oxygen, water, light. Living on sacred ground would mean that we have all the elements to support our spiritual life, an inner life where we can build the foundation of character, courage and awareness. If you are not grounded, you may create obstacles for yourself by being controlling, arrogant, defensive, worried, ambitious, selfish and afraid. When you are not secure in yourself, you may not feel that you have enough or that you have all the answers. But if you have the courage to stand your own ground, you can respond lightheartedly and spontaneously because you understand the process of maturing step by step. The key is building awareness and the ability to receive and to give selflessly. It allows the doors of the heart to open and overflow with Light. Everyone has the ability to recognize the Light within, regardless of the circumstances of your birth. Identify the inner and outer places that will nourish you. Recognize what you have gained in your life and its value, and have a clear intention to cut away old concepts that could interfere with your spiritual growth.

The kernel of learning – that remains consistent and accessible to everyone on earth – is an ability to go beyond ourselves and be of benefit to others. Accept your kernel and let it grow. The earth absorbs the heat and warms in the sunshine. Absorb the Light; let it fill your being. You develop sacred space within yourself when you care for your kernel of Light, just as the ground you live on becomes sacred when you honour it.

Ask yourself: How do I create sacred ground? What seeds nourish and support my spiritual growth? Take some time and space to do a Hatha Yoga practice:

1   Do the Plough pose, *halasana*, as a spiritual practice. The Plough pose is a tool that helps you prepare the ground for seeding something new.

2   While doing the Plough, think: Plowing the ground of my mind to make it open and receptive. Ask: What seeds do I want to plant in this ground?

3   Allow the insights, memories and creative ideas to emerge. Recognize what you have gained in your life. What treasures have you uncovered?

4   Write your reflections.

8 Coming Back to Harmony

THE WORLD THAT WE ARE LIVING IN NOW needs healing – the healing qualities of positivity, silence, relaxation, care, compassion and cooperation. We have daily reports in the news of people in pain, hunger and poverty, of killings, sickness and death. When negativity and greed tip the balance the world becomes an unhealthy place to live, lacking the physical and spiritual resources to care for people. We often feel helpless and separate from the rest of humanity. But remember that we are not separate beings, and we can consciously access the will to bring healing forces into the world in which we live and into ourselves.

In the Tibetan tradition there is an aspect of the Buddha called the Medicine Buddha, who is meditated on to activate self-healing. This Buddha's message is that our body has the capacity to cure itself from ailments. There is a healing spring deep inside that's available, constantly available. It gives us the opportunity to transform our life, to turn it around, to do the inner work and make healing changes. The Buddha's promise is that we can find out what is in disharmony and bring it back into harmony.

Coming back to harmony. What does that mean? Every person is unique, so there is no definite answer, but we can think of it as a sense of well-being, an ability to cope with life's challenges and possibilities, an integration of the good and the bad, the easy and the difficult. We know we are in harmony when we are courageous enough to yield and yet know where we stand.

The yogic practices are a means of clearing the mind and body, giving us the strength to be ourselves. The practices stretch the mind to incorporate the aid of the divine forces to help, to inspire, to surround and protect us. The tools available are light, rest, silence, time, movement through the asanas, sound and vibration of mantra, your own imagination and the power of choice.

Most people want instant results, but the practices are not instant. The practices and reflections are sustaining and designed to mature the positive seeds of Light within into a person who is truly human. It will be natural to be positive. It will be nourishing to be still. Relationships can be harmonious. Inner development is a long-term remedy, and the process of engaging in persevering spiritual practices will benefit ourselves and others.

As we begin on the path of healing, we will discover calm, focus and a clear mind to enable us to act from highest ideals. We can start using the knowledge we have with respect and gratitude. In a time of disharmony, can we remain without fear? Can we help and serve others without fear? How are courage and faith established?

The power in healing is that even though we are in a painful situation we don't flinch. We incorporate, we embrace. As we live through these experiences we note the pain and our reactions. We can resolve to be clear, to learn and do our best in the situation. Whatever we can do to heal keeps the learning positive and supportive. In doing so, we will gain a sense of victory and an understanding of what life is really about.

Yoga brings us to wholeness. The benefit of coming into health and wholeness through self-awareness is that we stop being just a body – needy, grasping, selfish – and become a living being in the process of gaining wisdom and compassion. When you do everything in your power to keep your focus on the Light, and bring the Light to each person in your life, then you are being responsible for your inner health and having a positive effect on those around you. The more positive view we can have, the more positive effects we can have on the world around us.

Light is a powerful symbol to send a positive feeling into the world, to people you know and love and to anyone who is in need. Here are three simple visualizations that can help you to connect with Light.

1   Visualize your heart centre and imagine a blue flame on an altar there. Take the flame and place it on the heads of friends, loved ones and any other people in need of Light.

2   In your mind's eye focus on a dot of brilliant white Light. Let this spark of Light flood your

mind, fill you entirely, ripple out to those who are close to you. Fill the place you are in, and spread it out to the community, the city, the country, continent, and the whole world. See everyone and everything in the Light and then draw the Light back into the space between your eyebrows. Sit quietly.

3   Sit and see brilliant white Light filling your spiritual heart centre. Open to a sense of generosity and ask: What am I grateful for? Desire to give generously to someone in need. Know that the more you give, the more you receive.

4 LIGHT

1 Living on a Prayer

I AM ON RETREAT FOR A FEW MONTHS, in a small, quiet place on the North Sea. It is similar to my ashram home on Kootenay Lake and yet there are different rhythms to life here – the sea tides and sunrises, the gulls swooping, the winds and their directions, the changing sky.

One morning, early in my retreat, I awoke with the words, "I am searching for Thee all over the universe" – a line from a prayer. It was still dark but a few brilliant red sun streaks rose at the horizon. I went quickly down to the beach. Watching the deep scarlet light grow was an awe-inspiring experience. A vibration started in the air and grew into a song. The birds banded together and began to fly with the vibration as if they were helping the sun rise up. Each wave was touched by red sun; the clouds and the air turned to colour, to light.

The prayer that was in my mind that morning begins: "From earth to heaven, I am searching for Thee all over the universe…" As spiritual searchers, we yearn for ways to connect with the Divine or a Higher Power, and we want to see evidence, proof. We aren't able to see the source but we can see its manifestations. Light is a subtle manifestation of divine power – and one that is universal to all traditions. It is a symbol, but it also has a physical reality, like the sun that rises each day, its warmth and light sustaining life on this earth.

There is also an inner Light that we can connect to, that sustains our spiritual lives, that is harder to see, but can be visualized as a vortex of Light within. It is often difficult for people to acknowledge that they do have divinity within, but this is a crucial part of our spiritual development. It may mean changing your idea of what "spiritual" is, making it more realistic, more human. It may mean accepting that you have goodness within you, and taking responsibility for nurturing your inner spark of Light.

Ask yourself: What would it mean to be sustained by Light? Light sustains that part of us that wants to have a life that is purposeful, meaningful and beneficial. It also cultivates; it is essential to our growth. We can grow into more harmonious, joyful, loving people. If you have an ideal – whether it is to bring harmony, to accept yourself, to really care about others – Light supports growing into who you want to be.

There are many powerful practices to connect to the Light. We can invoke the Light, see it showering down around us, we can meditate on images of the Light, we can see every cell of our bodies filled with Light. Light clears things up, like turning on a lamp, like a sunny day; it opens your eyes and reveals things you have never thought of before. My own experience of engaging in a Divine Light practice is that I had to accept change – change in my self-image, in what I could do and how I could be. This is not always a comfortable place to be. As you commit to a transformational practice, your ideals and generosity of spirit will be tested. Even as we yearn to be more caring and compassionate, we keep getting caught in our old selves and habits: we want things to go our way, we desire to be noticed, we expect people to do what we say.

On your search for the Divine, tests will come and you will keep making mistakes. But if you are dedicated to making these changes, you become aware of yourself and your actions. So instead of acting blindly, you act with an ideal in mind to be more caring, to accept your human nature. You can make mistakes, but they get smaller; you learn to forgive yourself. The Light sustains you through the process of transformation – you can invoke it, call on it, learn that you have a higher source of clarity and strength.

Over and over, at each stage of life we try to develop the courage to act on faith, to take the next step without knowing the outcome, without controlling how it should be. The Divine Light will sustain us in our journey. And we must sustain the practice. The more you visualize, invoke, meditate on Divine Light, the more it reveals and deepens our understanding that we do have a spark of Light within. We accept we are human and divine and we return to our practice to sustain us for the next challenge.

2 A Lesson from the Bees

A LARGE GROUP IS CHANTING *Om* and the sound coming from the room is sweet and harmonious. It reminds me of the hum of bees as they search for nectar, how ecstatic they get with their buzzing when they find and enter the open flowers. Some of them go from flower to flower, intent on getting the nectar; some fly off to tell other bees where the nourishment is.

Many people are searching for the nectar of spiritual awareness. Where do we get spiritual nourishment? There are many spiritual practices, many approaches to the Divine that are simple, nourishing and powerful. The first spiritual practice I was introduced to was the Divine Light Invocation. This is an ancient standing meditation that helps you visualize Divine Light, and get in touch with an endless source of spiritual nourishment.

I remember the first time I did the practice with my friend, who had just learned it at the Ashram. She was very excited. She had collected the nectar of Light and brought it back to me. I experienced lightness and openness the first time I did it with her. It was comforting and challenging and I wanted to find out more about it. Light is a powerful symbol, if we think of how even the smallest light will light up a dark room, stars from millions of miles away shine brightly in the night sky, and how we are dependent on the sunlight for this life on earth to exist. On a dark cloudy day, people can feel depressed; on a sunny day, spirits are lifted.

Yet Light is such a subtle, intangible substance. It is an image used to describe the indescribable essence of who we are. It is also a universal symbol representing a greater divine power. It is a source both within us and outside of us. Light is ephemeral, yet we can see it, feel it; some people even describe being able to taste it, smell it and hear it – all our senses can be attuned to it.

The practice of visualizing Light is very powerful and creates a feeling of oneness. Light has the ability to make changes on all levels of our being – physically, mentally and spiritually. You can begin to brighten your mind space and your outlook. Light brings changes to thought patterns and can also change the atmosphere around you. If you are in pain – emotional, mental or physical – concentrate on bringing the healing power of Divine Light to your body or your concern. Your Light-full attention encourages healthy thoughts. Negativity can be removed and lead to healing. The Light can also be sent to those in need.

Just as flowers are so generous with their nectar, the Light is abundant and always available to you. Once we establish a connection with the Light we can be receptive to its nourishment and generous with it too. We bring this generosity to the people we live and work with, taking the nectar we receive from the practices and translating it into our lives. These conscious interactions are the places where practice comes to life. If you visualize the Light once a day, you will begin to notice a change in your life. Write down your observations and your feelings. Your reflections will show the subtle changes and give you space to absorb the Light experiences. Then you have a record of how you are sustained by the Light.

Here is a simple exercise to visualize and affirm the Light:

Sitting in a meditation posture, aware of your spine and focused on the space between your eyebrows, bring your breath to an even rhythm. Use your imagination to see a brilliant white light showering around you and the Light flowing into your body through the top of your head. Concentrate on feeling the warm glow of Light suffuse your entire body, outside as well as inside.

Affirm: I am created by Divine Light. I am sustained by Divine Light. I am protected by Divine Light. I am surrounded by Divine Light. I am ever growing into Divine Light.

Acknowledge: Every cell of this, my physical body, is filled with Divine Light. Every level of consciousness is illumined with Divine Light. Divine Light penetrates every single cell of my being, every level of consciousness. I am one with the Light.

When you are meeting with friends, family or co-workers, mentally do this visualization and see them surrounded by brilliant white light, and keep the Light flowing around each person.

3 Dispelling Illusions
on the Path

WHEN I REFER TO DIVINE LIGHT I am referring to the
Essence, God, Divine Mother, Consciousness or Higher
Self. We need a symbol for this power, by whatever name,
that is greater than we are. The mind needs something to
focus on. Light is a good symbol because it has the capacity
to bring clarity or awareness. If you are reading and you
have a dim light, it's very hard to see the words on the page.
In order to see better, you get a brighter light bulb. In the
same way, if you bring Light into your life, you begin to
see your life more clearly, you begin to read it. Spiritual
practice is bringing the Light of awareness into daily life.

The Light will unmask your illusions. And because
of this, mental and emotional turbulence is not unusual
on the spiritual path. The path is not la-dee-dah. It is a
working through of our conditioning. It is a turbulent
thing; it has to be. We're on this human plane, learning
about being human. If we were perfect, then we would
probably be on another plane where everybody's perfect,
learning something else.

You start at the beginning with the human
condition of survival: anger, competition, jealousy, greed,

pain, fear. These things will inevitably be revealed by Light. This is the reality. Learn to read your life, take responsibility, because you will be shown what it is you need to do. You can choose growing into the Light or you can stay in the dark and grow more angry, depressed, self-important and deluded.

What does it mean for you to lead a spiritual life? What is realistic? If you liberate yourself from your concept of what spiritual is and get real about what being a human is, your life will take on a different meaning. If you take Eastern tradition without translating it into your own life, or you are rigid about Western religions taking their ancient ideals of meditation, prayer and austerities literally, you will be limited. When you go beyond the formality of the practices, to the Essence, to the Light, all the traditions basically say the same thing. Milarepa, Christ, Buddha, Swami Sivananda, Swami Radha, they have all taken life as a gift for learning. It's not about the robe you wear or living in a cave or a convent; it's about living with yourself and knowing yourself so you can be of benefit to others.

The purpose of spiritual life is to bring quality into life through the Light of awareness, understanding and compassion, not to get what you want or to be content in an illusion. People play games to get what they want on the spiritual path. Why? Because they are not committed to the Light and they are not serious about finding out who they really are. There are many games:

THE HONESTY GAME. You play at being honest, so honest that you're spectacularly honest. You can admit anything. Next week you can admit something else. The "honesty" becomes a substitute for change.

THE CHILD GAME. Acting as if you can't do anything for yourself, that you are "spiritually helpless."

THE HUMILITY GAME. You act very humble. Behind these actions there is a strong desire to be recognized as humble.

THE JUSTIFICATION GAME. Everything that you do has an excellent reason (for being done), so there is no room for the Light to come in. There's no room for anything to come in. The rational mind takes over, figuring everything out and making it tidy.

THE HOLY ONE GAME. Where you show all the actions and words of being holy but there is no generosity or consideration, only the appearance of holiness.

THE PSEUDO-SPIRITUAL LANGUAGE GAME. Using words like "transcendence," "cosmic vision" or "one with the universe." The words are a facade when people don't want to look at themselves; the language loses its meaning.

THE SPIRITUAL PARTNER GAME. Using your partner as an excuse to not go forward with your own evolution. You "wait" and "support" the other so you can both go together. Nothing

happens. Neither goes anywhere. What are
you supporting?

THE DREAM LOVER GAME. People often come
to spiritual life looking for emotional
gratification, a "dream lover" or "soul mate."
If you are not looking for your own soul, what
then is the purpose of a spiritual path?

One thing for certain, the Light brings pressure. You
might have the expectation that when you get to that
point of being lighter, life will be easier. But the Light
is bound to bring pressure. That's its job. Your faith
will be tested. You may get into a painful situation or
get despondent or depressed. Light will pressure you to
question your life, your actions and what has brought
you to this point. If you cooperate with the Light, it
will give you the ability to see through your illusions. If
you don't cooperate with your own evolution, or ignore
the Light, things become worse. Look at your everyday
situation. Is there tension, disagreement, conflict?
The Light will create this dissonance when change is
needed. This isn't a bad thing; it raises an awareness that
something has to be addressed. Will you just let it go,
avoid the situation? Would that be compassionate?
    Compassion isn't "niceness." It can be fierce.
The most compassionate action is to break the cycle of
illusion. Illusions are built from unrealistic expectations.
They create a sense of a false reality. That's the thing with
the Light, it keeps breaking the pots. Krishna breaks
the pots and keeps things moving, so your life doesn't

become a museum. He frees the rich butter to become available instead of being hidden away.

You can ask for the Light of understanding to reveal what you need to see in yourself and it will happen. Reality takes on a different form. The Light keeps breaking the illusions and bringing us to a subtler and subtler place inside ourselves. It becomes the building block. Can you see what really is and not just what you want to see? Reality is always better than an illusion.

4 Walking through Darkness

GATHERING MY COURAGE, I take off my shoes and step into the dark entranceway of the temple. I hold onto a railing made of large round beads that immediately reminds me of my mala. I take the first steps down the gradual slope. There are people in front of and behind me. I hear their soft steps and their breath but in the darkness I can't see anything. The way is longer than I thought and the darkness is deep.

Finally, I turn a corner and see a soft light shining on a huge round stone with an *Om* sign carved on its centre. It is breathtaking and amazing! The stone is smooth from the many thousands of hands that have touched it for a blessing. I rub the stone too and walk around it, then continue up to an exit, holding onto the mala railing. Up and up with each step it gets lighter.

I step out into the streets of Kyoto. This is my first visit to Japan. As I visit each temple I am aware of the play of light and dark – the shine on the worn wooden walkways, the soft glow of the dark green moss gardens, the shimmering touch of a golden roof reflected in the deep water.

Often, travel and new surroundings can force us

to be a little extra present. By experiencing where we are in our travels, we gain a different perspective on life "at home." Most of the time our own spaces feel familiar and ordinary. In new places, ordinary daily events are more involving in their newness. We readily enter into the unfamiliar and unknown to learn.

Can we take this attitude into the everyday? Each day we journey into unknown territory of ourselves. It's important to take in the whole spectrum of life, appreciating the dark and light.

Divine Light can show what has accumulated in the darkness of the mind and heart. We create familiar ways of being in our ignorance. We defend them in the darkness of our self-centredness, cleverness and pride. In a flash of Light they become visible like the junk in a forgotten cellar. Once we see what we have stuffed away in our unconscious we can start cleaning it up by bringing the Light in. The illusions that keep us from our potential have to be sorted out.

Do you know the uncharted dark places where there are fears, anxieties and judgements? Where do these images and thoughts come from? We can enter in with curiosity and interest. Who is the guide there? What is happening? What is the message? Can you suspend judgement and allow yourself to experience what is there in the darkness?

Spiritual practices, such as awareness through reflection, are needed, especially if life is difficult and when there is pain and disappointment. We are not daydreaming about liberation from our fears but taking the action to search for the Light even in the darkest moments. We know, having experienced the glimpses, we can find the place again. We can practise keeping the memory of Light alive – recall the highlights of the journey and how even the most difficult events can be turned around if we learn about our inner spiritual strength. Each step takes us closer to our inner selves.

It's amazing to see the transformation as people build a bridge to their divinity after suppressing the pain of abuse or abandonment. The strength of their inner voice gradually gives them a way to begin to deal with the pain.

We need to be ready to take responsibility for ourselves. We need to know we can enter the darkness and survive with the Light securely part of us. There are many paths leading us to the spark of Light within. Each culture creates whatever form, image or practice helps us return to our original purpose. Our life is impelled to keep growing and evolving toward higher levels of consciousness.

Returning home, imprints of the experience in Japan stay with me. As I walk into my home it is like a new country. With so many languages to learn, different ways to be, different ways to worship, why do we live the way we do? Can we consciously take the steps that lead us beyond our limitations and be open to new ideas?

The experience I had in the temple, walking into the unknown, echoes the journey of life. We have all walked through the dark times and found the moments of Light. When people study themselves, through yoga, at first there is an apprehension of what they will find, but there is also the hope that the Light will be there.

Everybody holds a fear of what they will find on their spiritual journey, but there will also be signposts to keep on. The railing, the guide, the practices. Step by step.

Every day the opportunity is there to step into who you really are. Keep going in. Embedded in each person is this seed of Light that nourishes, vibrates the potential. What is the clutter? What is the fear? Here and now is the time to start the journey inward and keep coming back to that place of Light.

5 Light on Family

WHAT IS IT ABOUT FAMILY RELATIONSHIPS that affects us
so much? I think of a friend, a man in his fifties, sitting
in front of an image of Mother Mary, crying, wanting
to be held because his own mother didn't hold him; of a
young woman I know who is driven in her work to please
a distant father; of a mother who feels guilty, afraid she
doesn't have the energy to care properly for her baby.

Whether you are a daughter, a son, a mother,
a father, a brother, a sister, a cousin, a grandparent...
everyone is part of a family. Family is a fact of life, and
experiences in our families impact us deeply, creating the
foundations of our identity. The habits we form in our
families stay with us throughout our lives. And, as we
all know, no family is perfect – but they can be a perfect
place to learn about who we are and how we interact
with the world. However, we usually find something
wrong with our family. In our ignorance we look for an
imaginary ideal version of life. Faced with the reality of
learning how to communicate, share, care and survive,
we create a lot of pain.

A family is a series of relationships, many of which
centre on the abuses of power or lack of love. Everyone

wants some love and power, but these are two very important words that need clarification, as we often have a limited idea of what they are and the responsibility that goes with them. Love has many expectations attached to it, and when they are not fulfilled there is disappointment and pain. If we are confused and unfulfilled in our life, there is a tendency to demand love from others, thinking we have that power. We use people for our own needs instead of caring, respecting and empowering each person in the family.

If you want to come to terms with the reality of your family, you need the wisdom to step back and see a bigger picture. Everyone in the family needs time to see how their own actions can affect others. There is a need for space and a time for communicating what is happening so assumptions and resentments do not build up. How do you resolve these while they are still small? What is each person's responsibility? Do you blame others? Are you impatient? Can you stop getting lost in habitual responses and old hurts? How do you start?

I came to yoga, as most of us do, at a difficult point in my life – my marriage needed help at the time. The most helpful guidance I received was to start changing the way I identified with myself as a wife and mother. Swami Radha spoke to me about my responsibility to cultivate the Light within me. She suggested that I begin seeing the people and myself in my family as more than our designated "roles" of mother, son, daughter and husband. My practice was to visualize my family and myself filled with Divine Light, surrounded by Divine Light. The Light gave me clarity to see the best in each person and help to understand that they each have their own path.

When I first began to do this it seemed very difficult to change my identification and I wondered what would I lose, who would I become? I had a firm commitment to an image of family. Did I have the strength to be on my own? As my children and I became more independent, I felt I was uprooting an established tradition. But, as I continued to practise, a lighter view of my life came into focus. I was able to see the images of myself that I had created and held onto, a mother, a daughter, a wife, and I was able to step more fully into who I truly was, without the excuse of or the dependency on that identity.

We need to realize that our family is not responsible for us being unable to do something in life. Some people use their families as an excuse not to step into the intangible spiritual study of themselves. You may have to change your cherished stories that hold your family in a certain role. You can't blame your imperfect father for a comment he made when you were young and hold him responsible for why you can't fulfill your potential. By taking a longer view, you will see that one relationship out of an entire life shouldn't be able to determine its course. By taking the responsibility to bring in the Light of understanding and to restory family situations you make change possible. This can empower you and help your whole family as you recognize what you have been given, what they have given.

The value of family often becomes more evident as we mature, as we create families of our own. I think of what my own mother did in our family of eight. It is more than I could imagine as a child. It was only after I had my first child that I appreciated what she had gone through – the day after day after day commitment – it is certainly amazing and exhausting. It is important not to leave the idea of family in the realm of white wedding gowns and smiling babies and cozy home nests. It's real work. Not every person becomes fully formed as a parent and not every child is wanted. It is also important to recognize what it takes to build a firm family foundation so that everyone is able to learn how to make his or her own decisions – based on an inner authority, not a perceived familial authority. It takes work and is sometimes a life's work, to become self-disciplined, overcome selfishness and the desire to control others, and learn to acknowledge the Light in those around us.

When the Light of understanding deepens, the young woman struggling to please her father is able to let go of the need for approval and find her own reason and talent in her work. The man crying with Mother Mary will realize that even though his mother couldn't care for him in the way he wanted, a higher power was taking care of him the entire time. The young mother restores her energy in quiet moments, breathing in time with her baby, knowing she connects on another level and is doing her best.

Your own family can be your place to practise selfless service and develop the qualities you aspire to and that will inspire others. In family, we have the intensity of a close-knit group with all our humanness exposed. We can bring in patience, care and understanding.

We can learn to love without attachment. The world needs this. The choice is there. Choose to identify with something higher – don't keep it a secret – there is so much more we can become.

6 Source of Wisdom

COMMITMENT IS AN ESSENTIAL FOUNDATION for spiritual
life. A good way to illustrate this is through an ancient
yogic story of two friends who worked in the field
of their guru. They spent day after day sowing seeds,
weeding, watering and harvesting crops. One friend
decided that the work was too menial and left, looking
for a better teacher. The other stayed, working in the
field and serving his guru. Over the years the friend who
left grew old and despondent with life. One day he heard
about a great and wise teacher who was helping many
people and he decided to travel to meet this teacher.
When he got there it turned out that this teacher was his
old friend! His lifelong commitment to service was the
source of his wisdom.

When a commitment is made on the spiritual
path, ultimately it is a commitment to finding the
divinity within. Perseverance is needed to dig deep
enough to establish faith and receive grace. If you were
digging a well, you wouldn't dig a number of shallow
holes, you would keep digging in one spot until you
reached water. People who have worked to find this
source of inner wisdom can be very inspirational.

And while we find committed people to be inspirational, many people resist commitments in their own lives. They are afraid that a commitment will hold them in a small space and force them to do things they do not want to do. But the power of commitment is neutral and the promise of commitment is that it can manifest anything. So what are you committed to? What do you want to create in your life?

We see that people who are committed to money know how to make money. People who are committed to their families have families; people who want to write or play music commit hours and hours to practising. These are all more tangible commitments, but you can turn the same attention to a spiritual life because if you want to do selfless service and access your inner Light, that also requires a commitment.

Commitment can be experienced in small practices such as devoting several minutes a day to personal reflection, or chanting or Hatha Yoga. But often people have trouble even making a small decision and seeing it through. We have to remember that we will build trust in ourselves by making decisions and sticking to them. Start with a small practice, something manageable, and stick with it for the length of time you decide on at the beginning. At times you may view commitment as limiting, but not using your decision-making powers and being uncommitted is also limiting. If you never exercise your ability to make a decision and stick to it, when you do come to a crossroad in your life you may find it difficult to make up your mind. Commitment requires both will and surrender: the will to stick to a decision, and the ability to surrender to that same decision.

Gratitude for the present moment supports commitments and can offer a way to act. Remember that it is not you who acts, and the power of the commitment will guide and support you. Then you can say, "Here are my hands, my thoughts, my heart. Divine Mother, use them today." Life is difficult at times, but we don't have to make it more difficult by indulging in fantasy and illusion. The power of commitment brings the stability to take life as it comes and can open you to the grace and guidance needed to move forward in a conscious way. By accepting the Divine and nurturing a new way of being, commitment becomes something you want to do, rather than something you are fearful of.

Tests will come to challenge your commitment and show you where you are in your ability to stay with it. Always remember your commitment – sincerity, perseverance and intensity will guarantee success over the struggles. There are sometimes clouds covering the sun, but the light is there – turn to the inner Light and do not let the mind cloud your heartfelt commitment.

Seeing yourself in a shower of Light is a symbolic concept of the Divine without. Realizing the Divine within demands another step of concentration and commitment. The "Pinpoint of Light" meditation will support you in this commitment:

Seat yourself in a comfortable position. Sit with your spine erect, and either cross your legs in the Lotus pose or simply cross your ankles. Rest your hands palm up on your lap. Quiet your body.

Now see yourself in a shower of Light. White, colourless Divine Light. For a moment think that you are trying to realize the Divine within and without.

Focus your concentration near the base of your spine. See a lotus bud slowly open and a tiny dewdrop, a tiny pinpoint of Light slowly emerging from it. See it floating up and up in the very centre of the spine. Slowly it floats to the place where the spine joins the head, and in a gentle curve like a shepherd's crook this tiny pinpoint of Light floats to the forehead and comes to rest in the space between the eyebrows. In your mind's eye see a flash of Divine Light illuminating the brain and all areas of mental activity.

After a few moments take the Light back down to its starting point, the base of the spine. Proceed slowly. Be aware of every part of your body that the Light passes through. When it has reached the lotus and touched its centre, the four petals close as if to protect something very precious. Stay quiet. Let it rest for a moment.

There is a knowing establishing itself in you, deep within you: I am not the body; I am not the mind; I am Light eternal.

7 Getting To Know
Your Inner Light

I RECENTLY LED A FIVE-DAY RETREAT with twenty-two participants. As people gathered there were mixed feelings of excitement and anxiety, wondering what they would find out about themselves.

Since each group requires a different approach, at our first meeting I put out feelers to assess the atmosphere: I listened to the voices as we chanted, and for themes that came up in people's reflections to gauge what we should focus on for the week. I know from experience that learning happens for both the teacher and the students. Spiritual retreats are not a static process; they are a meeting of many minds, engaging and ever changing.

One thing that I kept returning to throughout the course was the question: How do we learn? Sometimes we learn through life-changing events – a relationship falls apart, we leave home, work situations shift. Or sometimes our heart just opens in a moment of grace and we see our illusions crumble.

The opportunity to engage in spiritual practice in a group gives a gateway to more than just gathering information. Questions come up, such as: Who am I? What is life about? Why am I here? These questions have a penetrating, unrelenting quality. They are part of our quest to know more about ourselves and our relationship to the Light within us.

While there are endless ways of learning, learning about ourselves is a step-by-step process of building strength in new ways of being and thinking. Yoga is about practice and life is the school in which we practise. Life brings the pressure to look deeply at who we are. In the retreat, we took the initiative and time to reflect on our lives and asked: What do I need to know about myself, now, at this point in my life? Through spiritual practice and reflection, we created the space for inner knowing and wisdom to surface. In giving ourselves the time to do this, experience teaches us to trust our inner knowing, rather than some outside authority. From there, we can continue to move forward with an open heart.

Knowledge becomes very intimate when we become aware of the Light within us. Recognizing the Light within and seeing the Light in others, there is no right or wrong, male or female, teacher or student, old or young; only people with common experience and wisdom. There is no separation. Everything is supportive and we recognize the paradox of being human, with both failings and divine qualities. It is hard work to break free from old concepts and ideas about who you are. You must allow a shift in perception to occur. This is what I witnessed in the retreat as the students' experiences with the practices allowed them to begin to trust their own knowing – for each person, it was as if a layer of dust had been lifted from an inner diamond and the Light shone through.

Learning about yourself develops a flexible, expanding mind that recognizes there is more of you – more subtle levels, more understanding. Gratitude comes from that place of knowing.

Here's a practice that we used in the course:

1   Sit in a meditation posture. Rest your hands, palms up, on your lap. Focus on the space between your eyebrows.

2   Try to think of yourself without the body or face; in other words, avoid the familiar reflection seen in the mirror.

3   Visualize your body as empty or hollow like a glass bottle.

4   See a stream of white Light flowing down the centre of the form, filling the feet, legs, trunk, arms, neck and head.

5   Hold this image (a mass of Light in the shape of your body) for as long as possible.

Filling with Light can change your whole world because it changes what you identify with. Who are you? What is the image you hold of yourself? What is in your mind? This practice will give you a sense of the Light within you and you can experience it, feel it, see it and hold it.

8 A Skylike Mind

IT IS A HOPEFUL SIGN that the sun came out today after a long period of rain and overhead clouds that reached down to the lake. Light streams in through the window and the blue sky is expansive. Sunshine warms the room, and I have the desire to vacuum, tackle the cobwebs, dust the bookshelves, wash down, sort through, tidy up, rearrange, file and put in order. When I finish the room feels new, fresh and spacious. I sit. A quiet, open and peaceful space has been created that reflects the sky.

On a physical level, this light-filled space reminds me of what I want to do with my mind. I want to create a luminous mind. We spend so much time identifying with the busy mind, the monkey mind, the restless mind, all the names we label it with. We focus on the limitations, rather than the potential. We try to control it, overcome the negative tendencies, but what if we let the Light in? What if we recognized our minds as Light?

What is the mind? That is the first question you have to ask and explore for yourself. The mind takes up a lot of space and interprets everything you experience. In that way it is known as the sixth sense, interpreting all the information gathered by your senses. It is a great tool; it can take in all this information and make it into a decision, an action. It can learn and contain knowledge.

And the mind is very malleable. We can train it, through breath or mantra, to be in a space that is in harmony with the rhythm of the universe. And while control of the mind will not in itself lead you to an enlightened space, it helps you to get to know the mind, so that there is a way to guide it, use it to dispel the obstacles and to allow the Light to shine in.

When the Light lights up your mind, first you may have to address what it reveals – all the fears hidden in the dark, the issues left unaddressed – and clean up the clutter. And with the space that emerges, you may then experience a different kind of fear, what you could call a holy fear, a fear of the unknown, luminous mind.

To face the awesome part of ourselves is a difficult thing to do. We live in a mundane reality, and to go from the mundane to the unexplainable is a huge step for the mind. You will find that you are asking new questions, such as: Who am I? What is my responsibility, knowing that this luminous place is possible?

There is an innate desire in us to find out who we are. We may never really know the answer. Or we may never know how to explain the glimpses that we receive. Fear of the unknown can trap us into a resistant attitude and most people function below their potential because of fear. But remember that the mind has powers to continually manifest creativity and we can use this function to imagine beyond our limitations.

It is important to develop a daily practice of focusing the mind on mantra, breath or Light. At the beginning your mind may need to warm up to the concentrated effort, but then the mind settles in its space and eventually becomes familiar as this point of concentration expands. Sacred space is created, and you are sustained by the simplicity of it and protected by your sincere desire to know yourself. It is handy to have a journal to write experience, outcomes and the inspiration of each day, so you remember and start to identify with those luminous times.

Return to the glimpses of who you are and use your potential to the fullest. Bring the Light with you into the day.

This is what yoga is all about – building awareness of the Light and building the courage to live life. "I am not the body. I am not the mind. I am Light eternal." Make the space available – have a skylike mind that holds the Light.

5   HEART,
   DEVOTION,
   DIVINE MOTHER

1 Following the Heart's Desire

A BEAUTIFUL PEACE ROSE BUSH grows beside my house. For the last few years its branches have spread wildly, but were not producing many roses. This year it was covered in bugs. I began to prune it back so it could regain some of its vitality and hopefully avoid insect infestation. I cut and cut until there was only one stem left, and then with resignation I cut that too. A couple of weeks later a strong, healthy stem shot up out of the stump and very shortly had four beautiful blooms. It made me realize the strength of the rose bush. When the life force was given an opportunity, true beauty arose, unimpeded by wandering branches and bugs.

For your own life to bloom, a decisive action of clipping back is often required, a renunciation of the things that prevent you from attaining who and what your potential really is. Yoga is a path of developing awareness in your actions and thoughts. When you become more aware of who you are, you can then discern what will nourish the seed of divinity within. You may discover that things you thought were important will drop away, or that you are ready to clip away unnecessary concepts.

Many of us start on the spiritual path because there is a heartfelt desire to connect to the Most High and find peace. Following your heart's desire requires a willingness to make a commitment that will take you through the ups and downs. There will be obstacles on this path. One part of the mind wants to bring focus to your life direction. Another part of the mind questions and doubts. Is renouncing like rejecting and denying life? What will others think? What do I renounce?

People often think that by renouncing you forget the world, and live a peaceful existence away from the humdrum of everyday life. Actually, renunciation is learning to face life squarely for what it is and accepting responsibility for what you create. By focusing on the ideal of your life's purpose, you allow space for the essential truth of who you are to emerge.

Peace of mind doesn't necessarily come with money, a beautiful home, job or relationship. The mind becomes peaceful when a decision is made to be selfless, generous, forgiving. First of all, you have to look at what you don't want in your life. Are you greedy? Do you manipulate situations so you look good? Are you afraid, and try to control people and situations so the worst won't happen? Do you keep resentments, grudges and anger toward people in your family and community?

We have a responsibility to practise renouncing, letting go of the worlds we keep creating – mental, emotional and spiritual worlds. Can you renounce physical attachments you have created, the mental and emotional habits you have developed, and even the spiritual fantasies? What is your world and what have you built? Is it the world you want to live in? In renouncing the aspects that are not essential for growth in your life, a new sturdier, healthier, more positive way becomes possible. You want to be able to step to the edge in compassion and kindness, to be in the moment instead of being caught in the negative, critical or irritable parts, remembering past hurts or imagining future fears. Renunciation is also learning to trust that when things are let go we will be given what we need. We develop trust by suspending our judgements, releasing doubts and seeing what is really happening. The challenges are not obstacles. As you grow in strength, you will have the courage to step into the unknown. Renunciation requires a willingness to care deeply, accept yourself and use your intelligence.

When I think of renunciation, the metaphor of pruning keeps coming to mind. Each year in spring we prune the wildly sprouting fruit trees back to their essential unique shapes. The art of pruning requires us to listen to what each tree needs. Each cut is thought out and made in response to the tree's unique form. Well-pruned trees stand like joyful dancers, their branches free and open to the light and air.

Think of your life, think of what kind of person you want to be and what makes your life worth living. You need the courage to cut away what stands in your way of accepting your full potential. Find the subtle mystery within yourself, and behind everything the fragrance in the rose, energy in the sun, beauty in the world around us. Discover the design....the divine design in every moment. At times it's very clear, and other times you have to give up your need to control in order to recognize the vision.

In the Katha Upanishad, there is a wonderful message from the Lord of Death about renunciation:

"I've offered you every pleasure, fame, fortune and even a place in heaven and you rejected them all. Draw near now and hear me. That Self which you wish to know which is subtle and difficult to see is there. Deep within the deepest part of you, fix all your thinking and all your inquiry on that ancient, radiant Self. Through It you will rise above both joy and sorrow. Having heard this Truth, you must embrace it completely. Continue separating the Eternal from the ephemeral and you will attain full realization of that more inner, most exquisite Self, the source of true joy. You are ready for this experience. Now walk the Path of Grace."

2 The Divine Moment

IN THE BHAGAVAD GITA, Krishna says: "Fix thy mind on Me: Be devoted to Me; Sacrifice unto Me; Bow down to Me; Thou shalt come even to Me; truly do I promise unto thee for thou art dear to Me."

The Gita brings together the yogic paths of action, devotion and knowledge, all of which must be blended as we move forward in the evolution of our consciousness. Krishna gives us the choice to actively use our minds to turn toward the Divine: "Fix thy mind on Me." He is encouraging us to experience the Divine in every present moment. So, instead of letting the mind wander to the turmoil of the past or future, we can engage in what is essential right now. This spontaneity brings life to our actions and interactions; it can bring our lives to life. In the Gita, Krishna says that the ultimate goal is to live life and face death with the thoughts of the Divine on your mind.

I thought of this recently, as I sorted through an old trunk that had been stored under the house for over ten years. The items inside were all very familiar. Each one held a string back to a former life, tying my mind to old memories of forgotten people and places. I decided to give everything away. I wouldn't be able to take those items with me at the end of my life, but where do the memories go? What do I want to remember? What from this life do I want to hold in my mind?

The stuff of the mind is so subtle compared to concrete items that are easily given away. When I follow the memories back, I realize the mind holds the even subtler substance of learnings from those experiences. Through reflection and spiritual practice, the learnings of life can be extracted. Keeping the mind focused on the Divine – the Light, a mantra, an image of a god or goddess – can bring us closer to the essence or divine play of each situation. These feelings of closeness and devotion also enable us to respond to each other with more understanding and compassion. This is the foundation on which we can trust and accept life events as valuable – without judgement.

In our work, our relationships and our daily life, routines easily set in, and everything we do can become very solid, immoveable and inflexible. We feel limited and dead. How can we bring life into our daily actions? Every moment is calling for change, giving us a chance to leap into the present. There is no need to carry a trunkload of stuff into each relationship or each action. Instead, focus the mind on the moment. Cut the ties of old hurts and memories and images and see the situation you are working with now. The challenge is to continue to create new memories, not be bound by old ones.

Can you make enough room in your mind for a heartfelt yearning for the Divine to reside? Just as old memories carry us back to our old lives, a yearning can carry us forward. A divine connection can create an openness that will keep exposing the purpose of life. Daily life provides the opportunity to gain new understandings, and with these understandings there comes an acceptance of life lived.

In the Gita, Krishna emphasizes again and again to Arjuna: You who are seeking the Divine are dear to me. His promise is that our effort will not be lost from life to life. Through our yearning and through the struggles of life, we will mature and reach our goal.

3 The Ripple Effect

THERE IS A CRESCENT MOON hanging in the sky, and
the sun is setting behind the mountains, casting a rosy
glow over everything. I'm taking in the view after a long
day of winter planning meetings. The peace I feel now
is a good balance after the day's busyness. People often
think that life at an ashram is a peaceful paradise, but
like any other family or community, we have to plan for
the future and find ways of working and living together.
Part of what we talked about today was how to keep
our community healthy. This is a key question in any
community or group situation because communities
are living organisms whose healthy workings need to be
taken care of.

When a community or relationship needs healing,
you can see the signs manifest in many ways: people
don't feel appreciated for who they are; they feel as if they
don't fit in; ideas and events become separated and the
differences between people seem more important than
their similarities; words, actions and projects are blown
out of proportion; gossip and rumours abound.

Whatever community we belong to, we need to
be clear about our purpose and intentions. A healthy

community needs the strength of commitment from the people involved as well as open communication, gratitude and devotion.

All community work requires personal work. And all of our inner work requires patience. If we want to have a healthy community, we have to start by making an honest commitment and showing respect for the place we are in personally. Personal reflection and a personal practice are great tools for this. You can start by sitting quietly for a few minutes, or chanting, or doing Hatha Yoga and allowing your mind to relax. Then take a few minutes to write down what is on your mind. Ask yourself: What kind of person do I want to be? What are my ideals? How am I interacting with others – am I being straight? By taking time each day to check in with yourself, you build the trust and strength to address what will arise with others.

When we know ourselves, we can come from a sincere and straight place in our interactions. If you find yourself wanting to get out of a situation, walking around a problem or not engaging with someone out of fear or uneasiness, think how you would like to be treated if you were in the other person's place. Bring it into your reflection and ask yourself: How would I do things differently next time? When the situation arises again you will recognize the opportunity to take a different course of action. This is part of the perfection of life. We see our limitations for what they are and realize that we can use our limitations to keep transforming and evolving.

This brings us to the healing power of devotion.

In the Bhagavad Gita, Krishna promises that those who are devoted to him will come to him. "Fix thy mind on Me, be devoted to Me, sacrifice unto Me, bow down to me. Thou shalt come even to Me; truly do I promise unto thee, for thou art dear to Me." We can translate this into our daily lives by asking: What am I devoted to? How can I create devotion, a heartfelt connection to the Divine? Through your commitment and devotion, you can come to know your true nature.

Devotion requires renouncing some of our desires and realigning ourselves with what is very important and precious to us. Like a small baby needs to be looked after in order to grow, our spiritual life needs the same attention, love, engagement and focus. If we're just starting out on this path, we can consider our spiritual life like a "spiritual baby." Looking after babies always requires some sacrifice of time. It is essential to take the time to have a spiritual practice. Through devotion to your inner life you will find that your awareness and caring will naturally expand and ripple out toward others in your community.

It is important to take time to be grateful for the relationships and communities we are part of. Gratitude and humility are greatly undervalued feelings that open the heart and help us appreciate other people and their perspectives. Take the time to recognize what has been given to you. Recognizing all the sacrifices people in your life have made to get you where you are today, you will see how precious life is.

4 War & Peace

OUR LIVES ARE CONSTANTLY SHIFTING, coming in and out of balance. Every step we take requires us to go out of balance in order to move forward. Sometimes this can feel like a dance as we surrender to the movement; sometimes we need the determination to walk straight into what lies before us.

As I write this the world is braced for war in the Middle East. We are balancing between the forces of war and peace. On the television, images flash of streets that are full of soldiers and streets that are full of people demonstrating for peace. How do we resolve issues as a global community? At this time in history there seems to be a desire to deal with conflict in an intelligent way so that no particular interest gets out of proportion. We are searching for oneness. People are finding ways to come together to speak their concerns, gather the facts and be informed. With all the different languages, we find our oneness in the universal language of prayer, Light and peaceful action. Grave situations make us think more deeply about our lives and what we can do to achieve peace.

We need to look clearly at the world we have created, and our own inner world is a good place to start. When we look within our mind, it seems we consistently separate and polarize. We conceptualize and judge ideas as good and evil, male and female, tension and relaxation. Yet when we explore and challenge these opposites we see the variations and degrees of meaning. Take, for example, the duality of male and female. Everyone has the male quality of intellect and the female quality of emotion, and when they are brought together in us we feel whole. Each side can move to meet in the centre instead of tipping the scales in one direction. When the opposites are too distinct, our centre doesn't hold a steady position – it shifts and spins, causing imbalance.

How do we maintain a position of steadiness? When we look outward at situations in the world, we often feel that we have no control, no ability to effect change. But we can go back to changing our world within – where we do have the ability to change. We can change how we use our intellect and emotions so that we are not swept up by outside forces. When we harness the emotions and intellect, we can gather facts and mobilize ourselves to actions rather than getting stuck in reactions. We can't stop war in the world, but we can change how we react to war. We can sit in silence listening to our intuition, in stillness facing what is before us and in reflection thinking deeply. And in those moments of awareness, ask: What is the Divine asking of me in this situation?

The Divine is asking us to take responsibility for the powers we have been given. We have the power of choice. We have the power to choose to identify with the Light in whatever form and name we attribute to it. Also there is the choice to discipline our minds so that we are in control of ourselves and do not give in to the temptation to control others. We can be examples by developing the qualities of compassion and understanding. In this way, we elevate our interactions by bringing quality into our daily encounters and we make our ideals very tangible.

As we mature spiritually, the subtleties of the everyday become more evident. We can feel the power of the Light; we can gain understanding of the way it works. If we send out vibrations of Light, we will create a different atmosphere in the world. Peace and Light will manifest. Many people are influenced. It may take years or lifetimes, but every positive thought and action has an effect.

We often think of the power of compassion as a feminine force, as Divine Mother. We recognize Her as Mary, Tara or Kuanyin. We pray to Her in times of need. She can be thought of as a power that is outside of us, but She also lives within each of us – male or female. You can honour and worship Her by acting in a compassionate way toward all creation. All the world is Divine Mother. Her love teaches us lessons through opposites, the negative and positive, the sting and the soothing comfort.

The most powerful love is to support and encourage others toward their highest potential. When there is an imbalance in the world, and we want to take the steps to move forward, it is love that will protect us. There is nothing so powerful as being able to see the

Divine in everyone you meet, to offer love and Light, to envision people living in peace within themselves and with their neighbours, to send out loving-kindness to all.

5 The Power of Speech

THE OTHER DAY IN YOGA CLASS, Johanna, a student, discovered that she had based her idea of her intelligence on negative remarks she heard when she was seven years old. We have all taken in the opinions of others about our beauty, our creativity, our body shapes and our abilities. We know the power speech has to stick in the mind and influence who we are and what we do. We see how in a few seconds emotionally charged words can affect us for years.

We all know the saying, "Sticks and stones will break my bones but names will never hurt me." And yet this statement sounds untrue if we really look at the power of speech. Speech can hurt and speech can heal; it can start wars or resolve an argument; it can encourage confidence in a young person or destroy self-esteem.

Why is speech so powerful? The power of speech spoken aloud or voiced in our heads combines sound and purpose. From the cries that babies make to ensure their survival to our ability to express the complexities of our emotion and thought, speech is our tool to navigate our world. Sound, tone of voice, pitch and choice of words can manifest many things. Through the power of speech, the varied and multilayered meanings of words, we have an incredible resource for communication and creation.

In yoga, speech is a feminine force called the Devi or Goddess. Speech is seen as feminine in acknowledgement of its ability to bring things to life. We constantly use the power of speech to create the world we live in – it can be boring, full of anxiety and disasters, or it can be full of joy and positive experiences. How you describe your life is how it will be. We are responsible for our speech and the effect these words have on others.

Each word that is spoken is a vibration of sound, and a vibration is never lost. There is a great responsibility in what is said and what is set in motion through our speech. If the power of speech is not respected, then the powers of conditioning and self-hypnosis through language and memories of language will continue to keep liberation an unfulfilled hope.

Yoga liberates us from limitations, even those limitations that others have placed on us. When Johanna began to question the purpose of her life and ask, "Who am I?" she started to uncover what she had held in her mind for so long. Through the practice of reflection she caught the negative thoughts and saw how she had accepted someone else's definition of who she was. She had a choice to continue within the limitations or to break free. She realized her negative image didn't belong and through language began to affirm her intelligence, her creativity and her divinity.

You are given a choice of how you use the power of speech. Reflection on daily events brings awareness of the words you use and how the words work in your mind, call up memories and ripple into your life. A prayer to Divine Mother starts with the line: "May all my speech and idle talk be mantra." Speech does have the potential to evolve from everyday idle talk to mantra if we bring awareness into what we think and say.

Mantra is the practice of the highest form of speech. One way to understand the power of speech is to establish a mantra practice. Chant the mantra with dedication, love and the desire to connect with the Divine. Sense the power of your voice and try to discover where the sound is coming from, who is chanting, where the words go and what is created in your mind and in the space around you. Through mantra practice you train your mind and refine your speech. By repeating words of power you begin to make a connection to the Divine. Mantra allows you to recognize the Divine in yourself and in other people, and to make your speech congruent with that ideal.

This life is the opportunity to practise. By repeating sacred words the mind and heart become filled with mantra and even your everyday speech begins to hold power. Then you have a connection to the Devi in her mantric form; she is always there encouraging and helping you. If you repeat the mantra, drawing on all your emotional force, you will passionately engage in the practice of life.

Speech has a tremendous effect on the direction of

our mind and the evolution of our life. We must respect and take responsibility for what we say audibly and inaudibly. By refining our speech we can also open to a sacred potential beyond speech, the gift of the Devi, the knowing of the heart.

6 Wave of Bliss

O Divine Mother
May all my speech and idle talk be mantra
All actions of my hands be mudra
All eating and drinking be the offering of oblations
    unto Thee
All lying down prostrations before Thee
May all pleasure be as dedicating my entire Self
    unto Thee
And may everything I do be taken as Thy worship[1]

HOW CAN YOU BRING DEVOTION to practical everyday
events? Devotion can be more than something you do
once a day or once a week; it can be an integral aspect
of daily life. Devotion is a link to the Divine. Divine
Mother is the goddess of devotion, she creates the world,
she gives birth to our spiritual life, and leads us to our
potential. She is the most accessible force, and our hearts
naturally lead to her. She manifests in many forms,
encompassing what is human in us and helping us to
become more human.

---

1   From Ananda Lahari [The Wave of Bliss], an ancient Sanskrit
    text in praise of Divine Mother.

Divine Mother is energy. In the Ananda Lahari, it says, "She is the energy in the sun, the fragrance in the flowers, the beauty in the landscape. She is the primal life force that underlies all existence." Ask yourself: Can I see her in my day? Is she in the stillness of a morning practice? Can I be on that wavelength where I begin to observe the invisible becoming visible? Can I respect the miracle of my eye that sees it? Can I see the life leaving the cut flower or observe my energy draining away in idle talk?

Devotion will be different for each person and must be experienced to be truly understood. I've had difficulty writing this article on devotion because the language of the heart is beyond words. I have seen glimpses of Her in my life and this experience generates a desire to worship, a desire to listen and look for Her. Yet how do we recognize the Divine when it is so intertwined with the everyday – with speech, action, eating, drinking, sleeping, pleasure?

The intention of devotion is like following a thin bright line of awareness that vibrates through our lives. The more we concentrate on these vibrations, the more we can step out of ourselves and gain a broader view. There is less self-interest and more curiosity about what a situation is bringing to us. Then we notice how life begins to flow. Devotion brings events and actions to life; otherwise work, practices and life have a mechanicalness and dullness.

Divine Mother brings things to life, destroys and ends things in time, arouses and subdues the mind to keep looking for the inspirations in daily life.

Bringing the mind back to a simple prayer, such as the Divine Mother Prayer, cultivates awareness in the moment. Thinking becomes more reflective; speech becomes truthful, clear, compassionate and fierce. By remembering the sacredness of action in work we can become openhanded, generous and willing to do what needs to be done.

Life is a wave. The secret is not to resist the movement because that leads to a bumpy ride or a stuck place. Learn to ride the wave. When we ride the wave of bliss we are connected with something greater in ourselves. We need our own experiences of who or what the Divine is to awaken the heart to a new, fluid approach and adapt to what this life brings us. We can also enter that sacred place in our spiritual heart centre where we have memories of those precious moments with the Divine. The storehouse of intuition opens and we gain understanding of many realities. The synchronicities of life give us these glimpses into how the world and the Divine intercept our realities. The wave and the depth of the water are not separate; the everyday world and the world of the Divine interweave and interact. This discovery is the wave of bliss.

The secret of devotion is to find what focuses your mind and keeps it intrigued, real, engaged and involved. It is very hard to keep the mind on something that doesn't appeal to you. For some people, the Divine is as real as their best friend and they can imagine a very distinct image; for others, she is the breath; and for some, she is as subtle as the Light. That is why within the spiritual teachings we have so many options and methods of connecting with the Divine. When I choose Divine Mother, she is the image that I have created in my mind. She is the perfect match for me.

Create what is most beautiful, most loving, most compassionate, the most of everything you need. You can call on her in the aspect that is most helpful to you. You are calling on that aspect of the Divine in you. Then you need to act from that place. Remember your practice is meant to be a stepping-stone to Higher Consciousness.

Here are a few ways to keep your focus on the Divine:

- Silently repeating a prayer or mantra
- Keeping your image of the Divine close
- Watching your breath in intense moments
- Looking for the Light in another person
- Remembering the surprises and connections in the day
- Remembering the positive and the victories of change
- Chanting, offering your emotions back to the Divine
- Creating an image through paint, colour, clay, etc.

7 The Razor's Edge

THERE IS AN OLD STORY in which Divine Mother, seeing how her people harm themselves through their own jealousy, self-justification, greed, pride and selfishness, begins to cry tears of sorrow. Her teardrops fall to earth and each one becomes a devotee, willing to do Her work, the highest and most blissful aspiration there is.

What is Divine Mother's work? She is the force of compassion and caring, so needed yet so often unrecognized in our world. She offers a creativity that destroys rigid thinking. She is receptive to new thoughts and can birth new ideas. We can become Her devotees by seeing Her Light in all of our experiences. When you can see Her life-giving rays even in desperate human tragedies, you begin to understand how much there is to learn and how fragile our existence is. It's important to give wholeheartedly back to life. A different vibration of gratitude is set in motion, a clearer way of looking at the world and the mystery it holds.

Create an image of Divine Mother in your mind, with an awareness that this is creativity at its highest. Most of us create through sex, through art, through work, through all of our actions. The creative force is constantly at work, so we have to keep clearing things out and being aware of what we are creating. The force behind creation comes through from the unmanifest – you can think of it as thought, which may seem abstract, but it has energy and becomes very real in some way.

If we put energy into thoughts, they become quite solid and sometimes it is very hard to get rid of a solidified concept. We ordinarily load ourselves up with concepts and stories and desires and wants and worries and obligations and resentments. All that power can be redirected for our benefit and the benefit of others. If we can be straight, considerate and caring, we can build the foundation for attaining the power of discrimination and compassion, which is the potential of humanity.

How do you create a firm foundation with Divine Mother and know that She too is on a firm foundation with you? Through your own personal spiritual experiences, you can maintain a connection with your spiritual self and that state of awareness where everything becomes clear. Things that seemed so significant become insignificant because you know there is something else that gives your life real meaning.

When you look back over your life, sometimes you may think, Why did I put all my time and energy into those negative situations and ways of living? When we are caught in places of illusion or delusion we are blinded by emotions. We don't understand what we have to do and we want it to look like something that we can approach and understand right away. But everything is a process; everything is part of a continuum.

Often we may want someone to tell us what to

do. But when we go to someone else we are giving them the power that we could gain. So where do you go? How do you make that connection to Divine Mother? How do you recognize and understand and change? My guru always said she could tell the spiritual evolution of a person by his or her willingness to change and follow it through.

Divine Mother will give us the illusion, and She will give us the liberation. These are her extreme gifts. We have to decide what we want. That decision can be difficult when we are constantly busy and deluding ourselves about what is important. We want to stop running from all these different places and to all these different things. Just go to Her feet – we are Her children and She will look after us. You know that a mother will do anything to look after her child, and so will Divine Mother.

If you really want to realize your potential, you have to determine what you want – the understanding, the discrimination, the connection with the Light, whatever it is. Turn to Her, gaze at Her, and make your silent request. Keep that thought alive and then wait, because the promise is that you will receive what you need in proportion to the movement you make toward Her.

They call it the razor's edge because it's all up to you, and you are always the one making the choices at each turn. The thing to remember is that She will always be there to lift you up, to put you back and give you another chance.

8 The Four Powers of Divine Mother

DIVINE MOTHER IS SOMETIMES THOUGHT OF as a being outside of ourselves or as an image to worship. But she is really the power within us. Her many aspects, that are given 108 names in India, represent different powers. Four of her main powers are wisdom, strength, harmony and perfection. What would it mean to manifest those four powers in our own lives?

How does wisdom manifest? Wisdom is a goddess within us and arrives as a thought form. We cannot demand her presence but rather must wait as she takes her time percolating from the unseen to the seen, from the unconscious to the conscious levels of our minds. Divine Mother, as wisdom, resides as an intelligence in the heart. Connecting with wisdom means connecting to the heart.

This divine intelligence emerges when we care enough to put aside our own petty desires. If we do not, then our hearts close down. When we are heartless, it becomes acceptable to take advantage of people, and so we see crimes in our own families, in our workplaces, on our city streets. We see unsafe schools and countries at war. Because so many people lack heart, we live in a world full of conflict, violence and war. If we return to the heart, to the feminine within ourselves, we can hear Divine Mother's voice. It is in this reflective place, an amorphous, chaotic place, where our ideals are incubated and our dreams arise. We have to be courageous enough to enter in and to allow what emerges from chaos. When we enter Her spaciousness, magical things begin to happen, shimmering within us. Gradually, she comes into sharper focus.

Her voice, which is the voice of intuition, has a different vibration than what we have been conditioned to hear. If we can open our hearts to Divine Mother, she will reveal what we need to know, but not always in the way we expect. Rarely does she come as linear thought. Something is constantly birthing through her, birthing through our minds as insights, and birthing through our daily lives as lessons and experience.

How do we manifest wisdom? We open our hearts and leave space in our minds for wisdom to enter. We recognize that life is transition and it is not in Her plan that we remain stagnant. We let the wisdom of each situation bring itself forward and carry us to the next step.

What is the power of strength? There is a story of a man who was in prison for murder. Everyone was afraid of him because he was so strong, so loud, so unpredictably violent. His father prayed for him constantly, hoping that he would at some time see the Light. One day a guard noticed an unusual stillness and silence from his cell and went closer to check. The prisoner looked dazed and then suddenly reached out to embrace him. The guard quickly withdrew, but then saw the amazing light of love shining from the prisoner's eyes. When asked what had happened, he said that Jesus Christ had come to him and asked, "What have you done with all the strength I have given you? If you would use it for my benefit, you could be of great help." From that day onward, there was a dramatic turnaround in the prisoner's attitude as he turned his strength to new purpose.

We can ask the same question of ourselves: what have I done with the strength I have been given? What will I do with that strength? What is it that brings my strengths forward? The strength needed to face life's challenges has to be exercised in the same way that a muscle needs to be exercised. Divine Mother provides us with the potential, but can we make the commitment to develop that strength? Can we live our lives fully, following through on what has been given? Often we get caught in self-will and do not even recognize that the challenges are her ways to help us grow and develop our strengths.

We each come into life with certain strengths: perhaps strength of character, or certain talents and skills. Have you ever wondered why some people are strong in one particular area? Could it be that through many incarnations we have been developing our specific strengths? Think how Mary would have needed to build spiritual strength over many incarnations in order to give birth to Jesus Christ, to give birth to Cosmic Consciousness. Creation of any kind requires strength. Look at the pain and effort it takes to bring something to life. We can ask ourselves: Do I have the strength to destroy the obstacles that stand in my way? What is the irresistible passion that calls on all my strength? What strength is needed to create a new world for myself? Do I want something passionately enough to break away from the crowd and to do what is best for myself, for my family, for my community? Do I have the strength to uphold my ideals?

The third power of Divine Mother is harmony. We can recognize harmony in our bodies when everything is working as it should: breathing, eating, running, working, singing, praying – the body, mind and spirit uniting in harmony. We also know that when we are feeling ill or distressed, things are out of balance and we have to do something to re-establish that balance. Sometimes it requires medicine for the body, calmness for the mind, and inspiration or joy for the soul.

Divine Mother needs a sacred space to be within us. Like our Temple of Light at the Ashram, the inner temple cannot be built unless there is harmony. A temple of harmony can contain the company of the wise. If there is no harmony, but only resentments and power struggles, there is no peaceful place for her to reside. Too often we see how people do not know how to live together, side by side. There is a desire to eradicate or kill that which is different. What gives anyone the right to kill a life, a reputation, a relationship? We can ask ourselves: How do I learn to open my mind and heart to new ways of being? Is there space within my heart for a new idea, a new concept, a new person, or do I shut down and dismiss each new form of Divine Mother?

Accepting and celebrating our differences within our families and our communities brings a sense that we are constantly meeting ourselves. I often hear the hum of Divine Mother at work when I am in a group dedicated to the purpose of cooperating with an evolving ideal. The work is lighter and there is a place for everyone. Everyone is treated as if they were Divine Mother herself. We need to entice Divine Mother into our lives through living in harmony.

What is perfection? Our daily ordinariness becomes precious when we become aware of how perfectly a situation emerges, benefiting all involved. Think of a perfect moment. What makes a moment perfect? Details, sincere effort, right attitude, openness, gratitude, awareness, beauty.

Divine Mother will do anything to make us realize our lessons, the steps we need to take to break our concepts and to stretch our boundaries, to uncover our unconscious knowing. This is Divine Mother's job, to make us understand. She can open us to the experience of seeing the bigger picture. We are part of all that is around us. This is perfection. She uses whatever means, joyful or painful, to teach. Pain and suffering are the realities of our world. Unhappiness, pain, loneliness, death – everything we try so desperately to avoid are exactly the gifts she is giving us so that we can learn and evolve. Through reflection we can see how the details of our lives perfect our understanding of ourselves. This is Divine Mother in action, leading us to a more fluid, changing mind.

Divine Mother has many names and forms, and each of us has many qualities to help us with our unique mission. Because Divine Mother is part of us, there is always a guarantee that she will be there to answer any sincere call. She has given us this life and these powers. How are we going to use them? We need to consciously bring wisdom, strength, harmony and perfection forward in our lives. Then, when our lives are over, we will have no regrets and no resentments. We will have learned what we came to learn.

9 Dusting the Goddesses

THE FIRST TIME I CAME TO YASODHARA ASHRAM was in 1977, for a course called Women and Spiritual Life. In the workshop we were asked such questions as: What does it mean to be a woman? What is the purpose of your life? We wrote down our thoughts and then we read our papers together. All the women spoke about their spirits and used words that were strange to me. At that time of my life I saw myself as a mother, a wife, a sister, a daughter, a teacher. I had a list. The teachers asked me, Is there anything more? And I thought, No, not really. I saw myself as the dismissible, the invisible.

Every night I went to satsang, and chanted mantras in the simple gathering. One night, I somehow felt I was being lifted up; or part of me was lifting up and part of me was staying there. It was as if I was stretching into Light. I didn't know what to do with that experience at the time, so I just put it away. But it was the beginning. I felt that maybe yoga was a way of finding out the kernel of truth about my life.

When I was growing up in the 1950s in small-town British Columbia, all the women worked inside the home cooking, washing, cleaning, having babies. At that time there were very few opportunities for women – you could be a housewife, a nurse, a secretary or a teacher. Women weren't ministers, doctors or professionals. All the books were still using "he" and "him." So who were you then as a woman? I left home to go to university in Vancouver and become a teacher. I met different people living different lifestyles, and I eventually found women who were interested in women's issues, who actually talked about what it was to be a woman. We were just beginning to find a language to talk about ourselves and explore womanhood.

When I finally came to the Ashram in my late thirties, I met Swami Radha, a woman who was a spiritual teacher! There were spiritual images of such women as Mary and Tara, and prayers to Divine Mother – it was really the first time I saw respect for the divine feminine. Swami Radha described Divine Mother as beautiful, powerful and creative. She told a story about how Divine Mother cried tears over her people, over how they harmed themselves through their jealousy, greediness, self-justification. Each teardrop became the creation of a devotee willing to do her work, to be a handmaiden of Divine Mother.

Devotion, softness and compassion seemed so lacking in the competitive, aggressive world I knew. I was used to being influenced by an outside force that was male or male-dominated. To find a place that was safe and encouraged a different way was mind-expanding. I realized that I was devotional and enjoyed connecting to Divine Mother, who at first, for me, was an image of

Tara, the goddess of compassion. And I could connect with this aspect of compassion in Swami Radha. Her words were direct and full of power. She allowed me to see my illusions and also encouraged my potential.

Swami Radha give a talk and she said, "Do the Divine Light Invocation once a day and see what happens in your life." She wasn't promising an explosion of Light! She was saying, "Wait and see. If you actually do this practice once a day, it will change your life." So I decided to try it, and I did begin to change. I felt more alive, for one thing. I was just coming out of my marriage, looking for new work, and I was stuck. What was life about? There had to be something more to it. I could read a lot of books, do a lot of things, have a lot of friends. But I wondered: How do I get to know people more? How do I make real connections? Coming to the Ashram and doing workshops opened things up for me. I got to know myself on a very intimate level. I could move away from being attached to my husband and others. I could take the steps to become more independent.

I kept coming back to learn more.

An ashram is a place where you can fill up. You can fill up spiritually. I think that the Kundalini system can tell us all about what an ashram is. Just like in Kundalini Yoga, you start at the beginning by asking yourself, Why am I here? Then you can imagine how you want to be. You can use your passion to get there. You can open your heart and look at the things that need to be burned up. You can learn how to listen. Finally, you can learn how to use your intuition – I think that intuition is the gift of the Divine. You have to ask for it. And then you have to do the work.

When I finally moved to the Ashram in 1990, I remember Swami Radha asking me, "Why did you come?" I said it was because of Divine Mother. She replied, "Oh yes, it's because it's better for you to be with people of like mind and to be close to Divine Mother. You need to be here." Yet when I first started out on this path I never had any inkling that I would live at an ashram in order to have a place for my devotion.

I remember the first time Swami Radha invited me to come over to her house and look after her many goddess statues. It was such a privilege! As I dusted and rearranged them, fixed them up and put flowers beside them, they all started to come to life. They really came to life! It was an incredible experience. I wouldn't have missed it for anything.

I did the same with my own statue of Tara. At the end of each day, I went to visit with her, and that became a big part of my practice. Tara seemed very real to me at that point. I had physical responses to her – although she was not there physically. Sometimes I felt as if she was holding me, or that she was beside me, or that she was saying things to me. I took steps to get to know her, and as I got to know her, I got to know myself too. My self-image started to change. I was making a real connection to Divine Mother, and I was also making a connection to Swami Radha – a person who could challenge me and was a bit scary to approach – but in whom I could see the qualities of Divine Mother, of Radha, of that awesomeness of the Divine and also that gentleness.

I'm sure I projected a lot onto Swami Radha, but I think I was also pretty clear about who she was. I was able to build my own relationship with her and with Tara. Through those relationships, I felt my mind changing. I finally felt that being a woman was okay. I didn't realize how the 1950s idea of "woman" had influenced me, because women were treated like objects, put away and possessed, limited. When I think of it now, it seems like a weird foreign time when everyone smoked and wore crinolines! Those images had to be dissolved from my mind and it was important for me to instead see beautiful and powerful women. All of those old images started to change for me by learning that there was another feminine power available.

When I came to the Ashram, I just had this feeling of "there's something more." And I think everybody feels that. I see when people come here, they say it: "There is something more." And they mean in themselves, and in life. I'm often trying to understand, what is a spiritual person? For anybody, from the president of a country to the person working in a garage, you need to ask: How do I keep integrity, vision and purpose? What does it mean to be spiritual? Why would I want to be better than I am right now? Or, what would "better" mean?

It's interesting to me that Swami Radha came to yoga later in her life, as did I. It shows me that at any point there is a different kind of life that can be lived. What she did between her forties and eighties was incredible. That kind of commitment to the Light lands on earth and it spreads to so many people. It's inspiring.

That's Divine Mother in action. I depend on Her. I depend on the inspiration of Her beauty, the Light, how things change and come dancing into being.

Resources

Yasodhara Ashram, yoga retreat and study centre
PO Box 9, Kootenay Bay, British Columbia
Canada V0B 1X0
(800) 661-8711
info@yasodhara.org
yasodhara.org

About the Author

SWAMI RADHANANDA is the spiritual director of Yasodhara Ashram in Kootenay Bay, BC, Canada. She is an inspiring example of the quality and integrity inherent in the teachings of yoga.

She encourages practitioners to live their yoga in daily life and to realize their potential through self-inquiry, service and devotion.

Swami Radhananda is also the author of a memoir about her time with her guru, Swami Radha, *Carried by a Promise: A Life Transformed by Yoga.*